THE ANXIETY PROJECT is a new musical that explores true stories of contemporary suffering, loss, struggle, alienation, friendship, brokenness, love, hate, and everything that comes with anxiety and depression disorders and other mental illnesses. The show combats the last great stigma and gives voice to the people who live it – using the actual words of those for whom this disease is a large part of their lives. At once poignant and touching, this new musical explores the effects of mental illness on our collective minds – and how ignoring it leaves ripples in our social existence. Inspired by real stories of real sufferers, The Anxiety Project tells the story of Avery - one semester away from her doctorate in Psychiatry. Her thesis involves multiple case studies on Anxiety/Depression. Avery has charts, spreadsheets, and file folders full of data. But the more she delves into each case, the more she realizes that numbers only tell half the story. When mental illness hits closer to home than she ever imagined, Avery realizes that clinical must meet compassion as she finds herself fighting the stigma and giving voice to those who need it most.

I0560819

2023 Official Selection for Music Theatre Educators Alliance New Work Collaboration Catalog

2018 Official Selection for The Phoenix Theatre Festival of New American Theatre

2017 Official Selection New York Film Academy Musical Theatre School New Work Development

"Powerful. Cathartic. Beautiful. THE ANXIETY PROJECT is one of the most powerful shows I have experienced all year"

- Rebbeca Rudnyk, YabYum Music and Arts, Arizona

"Dean & Brush's work reminds me why I love musical theatre - it is everything I think this artform can accomplish"

- Kevin David Thomas, Broadway's Les Miserables and A Little Night Music; Co-Host of 'Behind the Curtain' podcast

"The lyrics hit like a jackhammer. Nothing is off limits. There is no judgment here. Just real and truthful depictions of the darkest corners of the human experience. THE ANXIETY PROJECT is unapologetically candid - bearing its soul without any filters - sharing the most vulnerable of ideas and welcoming them from us in return. The show feels like a close friend. "

- Rebbeca Rudnyk, YabYum Music and Arts, Arizona

"THE ANXIETY PROJECT is a bold, dramatic and wonderfully introspective look at adversity, connection and the value of self-worth. This daring contemporary musical resonates with a timely, ripped from the headlines depth that makes for an unforgettable theatrical experience."

- Russell Florence Jr. , Theatre Critic

THE ANXIETY PROJECT

Book and Lyrics by David Brush

Music by Rachel Dean

Original orchestrations by Benedict Braxton-Smith

Uproar Theatrics

LICENSING & PRODUCTION INQUIRIES
Uproar Theatrics, LLC.
hello@uproartheatrics.com I www.UproarTheatrics.com

The Anxiety Project
Book and Lyrics copyright © 2023 by David Brush
Music copyright © 2023 by Rachel Dean
Original orchestrations copyright © 2023 by Benedict Braxton-Smith
Cover art copyright © 2020 by Jennifer Dean

The Anxiety Project is published by Uproar Theatrics, LLC
500 8th Ave FRNT 3, #1714 New York, NY 10018

ISBN: 978-1-968051-38-9
First Printing, June 2025

THE ANXIETY PROJECT was developed in part through Queen City Queer Theatre Collective (Lindsey A. Mercer, Founder), New York Film Academy (Kristy Cates, Department Chair), Rubber City Theatre (Dane Leasure, Artistic Director), The Phoenix Theatre Company (Michael Barnard, Artistic Director), Arizona State University Music Theatre & Opera (Brian DeMaris, Robert Harper), Alter Castle Players (Megan Wean Sears, Artistic Director) and Gotta2 Productions of Tokyo, Japan (Jin Nishimura, Artistic Director).

Additional support provided by the Herberger Institute for Design in the Arts and Michael P. Brush.

THE ANXIETY PROJECT: Original Cast Recording available everywhere you stream.

www.deanandbrush.com
@deanbrushmusic

BRIEF CHARACTER DESCRIPTIONS
(in order of appearance)

AVERY – Post graduate student in her final college semester completing her degree in Psychology/Psychiatry. Avery is methodical, numbers-oriented and feels science can cure all. She struggles when she cannot find the scientific link to explain the deeply emotional symptoms of anxiety and depression.

MACY – Avery's younger sister. Secretly suffering from extreme depression and manic behaviors. Unbeknownst to Avery, Macy has attempted suicide several times. Macy is reaching out to Avery but Avery doesn't see it until it's almost too late. Macy is caring and longs for companionship with her sister. Macy is easily angered and explodes quickly. Often feeling she is "always the bridesmaid," she does things for people claiming to not want anything in return but feels hurt when they don't.

HOPE – 16-year-old girl. ADHD, generalized anxiety, struggles with self-harm. Quiet sufferer. Obsessed with Robert Downey Jr. as he represents a new life for her – a life where she isn't medicated but the toast of the town, the wife of Iron Man.

ELIZABETH (Rachel's Mom) – Long time sufferer of A/D. Has made life attempts several times – grapples with self-harm. She tends to lash out when confronted and then when backed into a corner, collapses emotionally. Loves her daughter – but her illness keeps her from having a real relationship with her.

RACHEL – Elizabeth's daughter. Hard working, self-sufficient – been cleaning up her mother's messes for some time. She has it down to a science. Would love to just walk away – but can never quite do it, so she finds herself caught in the same cycle with her mother over and over again.

DYLAN – Charming, mid-20's, funny and somewhat nerdy sufferer of A/D. Self-deprecation and humor are defense weapons that he wields like a ninja. A validation seeker.

LAURA – A/D sufferer – has a great deal of hypersensitivity. Gets her feelings hurt easily. Continually feels alone. Feels she cannot properly express how she feels and that no one would understand anyway. Cannot maintain long relationships as she bails early before she can become a burden to them.

CHARLIE – Laura's boyfriend. Loves her very much. Frustrated that he cannot solve her problem because he doesn't understand it. The classic non-sufferer companion – carries the shrapnel of her disease just skin deep.

ANNIE – Mid-30's, manic depressive diagnosed, Bi-polar that keeps her awake for as many as three days at a time. Level-headed. Understands her disease. Married to Neil for some time now. She feels she should no longer hurt him and decides she needs to leave him for both their sakes.

NEIL – Mid-30's, husband to Annie. Loving, loyal, hurt, bitter. Has always been there for her, so her leaving him comes as a hurtful blow. It's an ending he cannot understand.

DAN – Generalized anxiety triggered by father abandonment at age 8. Medication and therapy is a way of life. In fact, he's doing quite well until his father re-emerges in his life 15 years later.

DAN'S FATHER – Deadbeat dad. Abandoned his wife and child when Dan was 8. Wrote a few letters, but largely has been absent. He is regretful, but too late – the damage to both of them is done.

CARA – Recovering alcoholic. Her intoxicated days led to physical and emotional hurt she is now on a journey to repair – as much as she can. Falling off the wagon is a very real possibility.

JOE – Cara's former friend (perhaps more). Joe and Cara spent a good deal of their time together while she was drunk. When Cara earned her first DUI, she and Joe severed ties. He loved Cara once – but is hesitant to bring all of that chaos back into his life.

ETHAN – A/D sufferer whose symptoms manifest in physical violence – especially against his girlfriend. He often fails to see or maybe even know the severity of his actions. That is, until his girlfriend Molly decides she's had enough.

MOLLY – Ethan's supportive girlfriend – who has suffered abuses both physical and emotional from him and has finally decided it's enough.

ROSE, ALICIA, & KRISTINA – Three women at various stages of their life with exact same diagnoses but starkly different symptom manifestations. They represent frustration for Avery as she constantly searches for scientific consistency.

AARON – Manic depression, medicated, ashamed. Loving, passionate – feels his disorder is a black cloud that makes him unlovable and problematic in relationships.

MAX – Aaron's fiancé. Loving, supportive – aware of Aaron's disease and loves him anyway. It's a non-factor for him. Max wants to marry Aaron, but Aaron worries that he will become too much for Max to handle. Max is the wisdom in the room when it is most needed.

AMY – Long time self-harmer, in a support and recovery group. We meet her when she is three months free of cutting. Amy's history is dark but represents an emergence from the pain – a pain-free life IS possible.

OTHER CHARACTERS:
Molly's friend
News Anchor
'Balloons' Therapist
Bartender

PREFACE

The first email popped into our inbox late one night. If we are being honest, we didn't expect to receive any responses at all to our blog post calling for stories. After all, we were asking strangers to share intimate details of their struggles with mental illness—specifically anxiety and depression—in a world that still holds a firm grip on stigma towards those who suffer. We had no idea, really, what we were going to do with these stories. We are not doctors. We are not psychiatrists. We are musical theatre writers. The trajectory of this journey had not yet revealed itself: this was the very definition of a shot in the proverbial dark. But the light of "New Message" in our inbox that night blasted open the door of what would become our musical THE ANXIETY PROJECT. That first email was intimate, personal, didactic, heartbreaking, thorough, and deeply revealing. We felt a bit guilty that we knew that much about a stranger, as though we'd peered in on someone's private life uninvited. But we *had* been invited, right? The story, together with many that followed, included tales of depression, abuse, self-harm, suicide, addiction, familial breakdown, marriage and divorce, sickness and health, rock bottoms and mountaintop climbs. They ran the gamut of emotional spectrums, but they were all linked by the indelible truth that strangers had shared their stories for one reason only: because they were asked. We said "tell us your story," and the dam had broken. The dam that held back a deluge of weight that desperately needed relief. That revelation—that people *need* to share their stories—marked the beginning of our first musical together. It should've been obvious, yes? After all, musical theatre is nothing if not a storytelling craft, and the brave yet private nature of these stories compelled us to action. We were no longer solicitors of stories, but harbingers. And as such, we immediately were indebted to these strangers. We owed them a voice. THE ANXIETY PROJECT became that vehicle. And now - many cities later - here we are - letting the show tell *us* where to go next.

Struggles with anxiety and depression are all too real and all too common. At their worst, they can be life-threatening. The process of writing the piece became a kind of therapy for us —a way for us to learn lessons from those who had been to hell and back. Among many things, here is what we have learned:

1. *Anxiety and depression ARE illnesses. And as such, they need to be addressed, treated, and communicated.*
2. *The very symptoms of the disorder (particularly hopelessness) are why most who suffer never seek help. Why seek help for something that seems hopeless, right? This is why it can be so dangerous.*
3. *The most important thing people can do for those in their life who are suffering is ask, "Are you okay?" And then ask again, "Are you really okay?" The second time is key. Being seen and heard is the goal, not being fixed.*
4. *The darkness of anxiety and depression is the terror. Lonely, abandoned terror. Fear is the enemy of our brains under normal circumstances. Under the shadow of these disorders, that enemy multiplies, complicates, and spirals.*
5. *The stigma surrounding mental health in general is reductive and ignorant at best and dangerously epidemic at worst.*
6. *Art heals. Art activates. Art incites. Art asks. Art demands. Our hope is that our musical lives up to these high standards to which we hold our very precious art form.*
7. *These are not issues reserved only for doctors and clinicians. We all have a responsibility to reach out and speak for those who feel voiceless.*

We hope the community created here is a place where you can feel seen and heard and know that you are far from alone. We hope, too, that as a family of humans, we can be the changemakers and trendsetters that bring an end to the stigma of mental illness in the world at large and that we are propelling forward to the day when *everyone* feels seen and heard and *no one* feels alone.

David Brush & Rachel Dean

Creators of THE ANXIETY PROJECT

PROLOGUE

> *(Entire cast in tableau. We hear snippets -
> prequels of stories that will flesh themselves out
> later. These should be dialogue (NOT lyric) clips
> of your choosing from later in the show and can
> be live or pre-recorded. Overlapping becomes
> more and more intense until it is just a
> cacophony of noise. Lines can repeat to create
> that effect. Noise then dissolves into the song.)*

CUE: TODAY (AND EVERY DAY)

> *(Entire cast enters randomly - circling -
> increasingly more frantic.)*

COMPANY (SOLOS AT DIRECTOR'S DISCRETION)

> *(Without MACY and AVERY)*

IT'S ALL IN MY HEAD IT'S ALL IN MY HEAD

IT'S ALL IN MY HEAD IT'S ALL IN MY HEAD

THE PROBLEM HERE IS ALL JUST IN MY HEAD

IT'S MONDAY MORNING - RAIN BEATS DOWN
MY WINDOW
THE STRESS BEGINS THE SECOND I LEAVE THIS
PILLOW
THERE'S A LIKELY CHANCE THIS DAY WILL
TREND
TOWARD THE WAYS THESE DAYS ALWAYS SEEM
TO END

COMPANY (CONT)
DEFEAT - DELETE - AND A SUDDEN RETREAT
IT'S A DANCE I KNOW TOO WELL
A SPELL I CAN'T SEEM TO QUELL

SO I'LL MOVE AT THE PACE I CAN
FORMULATE A SURVIVAL PLAN
I WON'T COMPLAIN ABOUT THE WIND IN MY
HEAD
JUST ADJUST THE SAILS INSTEAD
SAYING ONLY WHAT I HAVE TO SAY
JUST TO GET ME THROUGH TODAY AND EVERY
DAY

I CAN FEEL IT RISING UP AGAIN
DON'T WANNA BE THE WAY I'VE ALWAYS BEEN
SO I PAUSE
AND LET THE COFFEE DO ITS WORK
TO TAME ANY SOCIALLY UNACCEPTABLE
QUIRK
BUT THE FEELINGS STILL LURK BENEATH THE
SURFACE
SO I'LL SHUT THAT AWAY IN THE SERVICE
OF JUST SURVIVING THE DAY
AND I'LL MOVE AT THE PACE I CAN
FORMULATE A SURVIVAL PLAN
THE MONSTER THAT LIVED UNDER MY BED
IS RENTING ROOM NOW IN MY HEAD
SO I'LL SAY ONLY WHAT I HAVE TO SAY
JUST TO KEEP THE BEAST AT BAY ANOTHER
DAY

I AM WORTHY *(THAT'S WHAT I'M SUPPOSED TO
SAY)*

I AM WORTHY *(THAT'S WHAT THE PAMPHLET
TOLD ME ANYWAY)*

COMPANY (CONT)
HAPPY TO BE STANDING
HAPPY TO BE LANDING HERE
NEUTRAL IS THE PLACE I THRIVE
WHEN THE GOAL IS JUST SURVIVE

ONE MISSISSIPPI
TWO MISSISSIPPI
THREE MISSISSIPPI
FOUR MISSISSIPPI
FIVE - SHIFT THE GEAR TO DRIVE

AND MOVE AT THE PACE I CAN
EXECUTE THIS SURVIVAL PLAN
I CAN'T CURSE THE CONSTANT RAIN
CAUSE IT MIGHT WASH AWAY THIS STAIN
I'LL FIND A BETTER PATH - A TRUER WAY
JUST TO GET ME THROUGH TODAY ...
MAYBE CHANGE THE SKEW ...
NOW I CHOOSE NOT TO FLY AWAY
THIS TOO SHALL PASS OR SO THEY SAY
JUST ME AND THE WORLD - LET'S GO
LEARN THE LINES - PERFORM THIS WELL-
REHEARSED SHOW
TODAY AND EVERY DAY

(Button. Segue to Scene 1)

SCENE 1: MEAN TECHNICIAN

> *(A small one bedroom apartment within walking distance of the university. A simple desk with an open laptop. Papers, books, clothes and leftovers strewn throughout. A guitar rests on its stand in the corner. AVERY paces the room – the crust end of a pizza slice still in mid-devour hanging from her mouth. Her younger sister*

MACY is lying on the floor under AVERY's desk connecting a myriad of cords with both the ease and condescension of a Best Buy Geek Squad employee.)

AVERY

Ready yet?

MACY

I swear to God if you ask me that one more time…

AVERY

I was just checking if…

MACY

I'm still on the floor – would I be still on the floor under your desk if it was ready?

AVERY

You're a mean technician.

MACY

And you're a nagging sister.

(long beat. MACY continues to work)

AVERY

Did you plug the thing into the other thing or was it…

MACY

I will very literally punch you…

AVERY

I was just asking about…

MACY

About things you don't know about…love you…I do…but
you asked me to drive all the way here to 'tech support' you
and…

AVERY
(overlapping)
I didn't just ask you to "tech support' me – I wanted to see
you…

MACY

…now I just need you to let me do it...ok?

(beat)

AVERY

Ok.

MACY

Ok.

*(long beat. MACY gets up from the floor and
moves to laptop – typing away - continues to
work)*

AVERY

How's Mom?

MACY
(while she keeps working)
Catatonic. As per usual.

AVERY

You need to move out.

MACY

Ya think?

AVERY

So do it.

MACY

Are *you* gonna pay for that?

AVERY

Sorry…I just meant…

MACY
(truly – honestly)

I know.

(beat)

AVERY
(treading carefully)
I just worry about you…and maybe some changes in you
I'm seeing…I mean…you're different…or distracted…and I
just want you to have…

MACY
(getting up from desk)
There. All set. All you have to do is hit record, say the
brilliant Ivy League things you will likely say…

AVERY
(overlapping)
This isn't an 'Ivy League' …

MACY

…and then hit 'publish.' Peasy.

AVERY

Peasy...thanks.

MACY

No worries.

(awkward beat)

MACY

So – I should head out…

AVERY

Oh my gosh yes – You need to get back, right? Of course….
(beat- subtext: "I don't want to ask but probably should").
Are you sure you don't wanna stay?

MACY

(looks around the tiny apartment)
As comfortable as the bathtub sounds, I think I'll pass.

(they laugh – like sisters – like friends - like a
way they once were but is now lost or skewed)

AVERY

I'm sorry we didn't get to hang out more – It's this thesis and
it's final year and …

MACY

And you're still pissed at me for showing up blasted at Dad's
funeral.

(beat)

AVERY

(Shocked)
It's not..I don't...that was a long time ago…

(beat – MACY grabs her backpack and keys and
walks to door)

MACY

I'm sorry...just...I'm making better choices now is all I was trying...

AVERY

Text when you get home, OK?

MACY

(Subtext: "Of course - typical Avery - avoiding serious topics")

Sure.

> *(MACY exits. AVERY takes a beat – goes to the door. She has something else she wants so desperately to say to her sister. She opens the door – but Macy is gone into the darkness. A missed opportunity. Carefully, AVERY moves to her laptop and sits down - adjusts the microphone. "Testing 1, 2..etc". Once she is satisfied, she takes a swig of water – and takes a breath. She hits record. Podcast episode 1 begins.)*

AVERY

Ok…so hello – um…what do I call you – listeners – subscribers - *(attempting a joke)* voyeurs. Welcome one and all. I am Avery A. Hollisten – and this is my reluctant podcast documenting my final year – my SENIOR year. I should explain – I say 'reluctant' because I don't see the point of ALSO recording an 'audio diary' of my 'process' but apparently, I needed something else to do besides the 100-page, fully annotated, single-spaced, research-heavy case study document I need to complete my degree in Psychology….in 16 weeks.

Alright – if you promise to keep listening and keep the creepy comments to a minimum, I will try to keep my sarcasm on low boil. Deal? The case studies I will discuss have been...um…"names have been changed to protect the innocent"*(a la 'Law and Order')* - namely ME - from lawsuits I cannot afford. But I promise you this - their stories are real. Every detail preserved - which either means you have already stopped listening or you're all ears. Either way - here we go! So first things first. Who am I?

CUE: THINK ABOUT THAT

I am a 23-year-old college student – slash – happily single female – slash – superhero fanatic – slash – friend you call at 3am cause I will *always* answer – slash – dog lover – slash – cat hater – slash – all around well-balanced, high-achiever. I'm a semi-millennial – hence all the 'slashes.' I am not defined by just one thing! *(chuckles at herself).* Well – not yet – one semester away! Finally!

> THINK ABOUT HOW I'LL BE FREE OF
> PROFESSORS
> SLEEP IN FOR A CHANGE – EAT NORMAL FOOD
> THINK ABOUT HOW THIS ALL BE WILL ENDING
> AND MY REAL LIFE WILL FINALLY BE
> BEGINNING
> JUST THINK ABOUT THAT

One step closer to the corner office – the private practice – "Your next patient, Dr. Hollisten." "Should I hold your calls, Dr. Hollisten?" "Your private jet has arrived, Dr. Hollisten."

> THINK ABOUT HOW ALL THE WORK WILL BE
> WORTH IT
> NAME ON THE DOOR - DIPLOMA ON THE WALL
> THINK ABOUT APARTMENTS WITH MORE THAN
> ONE ROOM
> AND AN ACTUAL KITCHEN – AND A VIEW OF
> THE CITY

JUST THINK ABOUT THAT

THINK ABOUT ALL THE LIVES YOU'LL BE
CHANGING
THE PEOPLE YOU'RE HELPING
THE MINDS YOU'LL BE HEALING
JUST THINK ABOUT THAT

CASE AFTER CASE – FACE TO FACE
CHECK THEM OFF – ONE BY ONE
DAMN – IT'S GONNA FEEL GOOD TO FINALLY
WIN
WHEN THE DOCTOR IS FINALLY IN

I can do this - one ...more ...paper....one more step.

THINK ABOUT HOW YOU'VE EARNED YOUR
CAREER NOW
STEPPED THROUGH THE PACES – PAID YOUR
DUES
THINK ABOUT HOW THE LIFE THAT YOU
WANTED
IS JUST 16 WEEKS AWAY – GIVE OR TAKE A DAY
JUST THINK ABOUT THAT
YEAH JUST THINK ABOUT THAT

So – my thesis. My research will explore how data collection
and regulated case studies can lead psychologists and
psychiatrists to develop effective methods for both the
diagnosis and treatment of anxiety and depression-related
behavior and cognitive... *(stops herself)* ...ok I can actually
hear you falling asleep. Let's try this – *(she shuffles for
papers)* ...hold on I know it's....ah here we go! According to
the Anxiety and Depression Association of America, ***[18%
of the population has an anxiety disorder and only 1/3 of
those are receiving treatment. More than one half of**

AVERY (CONT)
**those 18% also suffer from clinical depression. Women
are nearly twice as likely to be diagnosed as men]**....and
the numbers go on and on and on. Science has cured our
disorders before – I am convinced it can again. So there you
have it – my semester – just me, all of you, a relentless thesis
committee – and the anxiety project.

***Stats should reflect current national information for
your production. Sadly, this changes all the time and of
late, not in the right direction**

> *(AVERY sighs as if to begin.)*

SCENE 2: RDJ

AVERY
Case number 5611P. Ongoing. Hope.

> *(The empty bedroom of a teenage girl.
> Nondescript. Quiet. Suddenly - a burst – HOPE
> storms in crying, distraught - she sits on her
> bed.)*

AVERY
16 years old. ADHD, generalized anxiety, depression. Well,
maybe. Poor response to medication seems to indicate a
possible misdiagnosis. But it's only been three weeks since
she began medication.

> *(She looks tired, disheveled – long day – and yet
> also wired – breathing heavily. She checks her
> reflection in the mirror. She has been crying. She
> kicks off her shoes – rummages through her
> nightstand until she finds a prescription bottle –*

*with which she carefully counts out her dosage –
and maybe one more for good measure. With the
water bottle on her nightstand, she takes them
all at once. She immediately begins to self-
soothe. HOPE puts in earbuds and immediately
the music begins.)*

CUE: RDJ AND ME

*(She pulls out a magazine and flips through the
pages.)*

HOPE
THINK ABOUT WHAT HE'LL SAY WHEN YOU'RE
TOGETHER
THINK ABOUT ALL THE WAYS HE'LL CHANGE
YOUR LIFE
THINK ABOUT SUN-DRENCHED SUMMER DAYS
WALKING ARM IN ARM TO CONCERTS, MOVIES,
PLAYS

IMAGINE WHAT HE'LL DO WHEN YOU'RE
ALONE WITH HIM
THE WAY HIS LIPS WILL FEEL AS THEY KISS
YOURS
HOW HIS ARMS WILL HOLD YOU TIGHT
AND HOW YOU'LL FEEL THAT EVERYTHING'S
ALL RIGHT

JUST THINK ABOUT EVERYTHING I WILL BE
WHEN ROBERT DOWNEY JR. KISSES ME

SOME GIRLS PLASTER POSTERS ON THEIR
BEDROOM WALLS SOME CUT OUT FACES IN
MAGAZINES
BUT THAT'S NOT THE KIND OF GIRL I AM

HOPE (CONT)
I'M NOT JUST A PASSING SCHOOLGIRL FAIR-
WEATHER FAN

I KNOW ONE DAY WE'LL HAVE OUR MEET-CUTE
MOMENT AND HE WILL SEE AS CLEARLY AS I
DO
THAT HE AND I ARE BOUND BY FATE
AND CANNOT RESIST THE PULL – NO TIME TO
WAIT

MAYBE I CAN FINALLY BE STRONG AND FREE
WHEN ROBERT DOWNEY JR. MARRIES ME

And then – naturally – our wedding day!

I CAN SEE MY GOWN OF WHITE
AND HE IN TAILED TUXEDO
FLOWER GIRL GENTLY TOSSING BLOOMS OF
ROSE
THE BAND WOULD PLAY OUR SPECIAL SONG
WE'D KNOW ALL THE WORDS AND SING ALONG
AND ALL WOULD BE RIGHT THAT ONCE WAS
WRONG BEFORE
A PRIVATE JET WOULD WHISK US OFF TO PARIS
WALKING ARM AND ARM ALONG THE SEINE
DINNER FOR TWO UNDER THE STARS ABOVE
FALLING MADLY, DEEPLY, AND ACHINGLY IN ….

(dazes off…lost in the dream)

(suddenly coming to)
THEN WE'D HAVE A FAMILY
TWO GIRLS AND A BOY – A REAL FAMILY

(sigh)

HOPE (CONT)
IMAGINE HE AND I WALKING THROUGH THE
THEATRE DOOR AT THE RED-CARPET PREMIERE
OF *IRON MAN 4*
THE PRESS WOULD ALL GATHER CLOSE
AROUND
AND ASK ABOUT THE NEW BEAUTY ROBERT'S
FOUND

AND I WILL BE THE BEAUTY THEY SEE
WHEN ROBERT DOWNEY JR. CHOOSES ME

(grabbing the bottle of pills)
AND I WILL NOT NEED THESE ANYMORE THE
DAY RDJ COMES THROUGH MY DOOR
NO ONE WILL THINK I'M SICK OR WEIRD OR
BROKEN
WHEN ROBERT DOWNEY JR. SAYS I DO
JUST US AGAINST THE WORLD
YES ROBERT DOWNEY JR. – ME AND YOU

SCENE 3: BLOODY TOWELS

(ELIZABETH appears holding a file folder.
AVERY does not acknowledge her.)

AVERY
Case number 4938E. Ongoing.

ELIZABETH
(subtext: 'um…I have a name' – hands over her folder to
AVERY.)
Elizabeth.

AVERY

Female, 43. Exaggerated OCD with tendencies toward bi-
polar.

ELIZABETH
(chuckles – with sarcasm)
Yeah – 'tendencies.'

AVERY

Infrequent therapy – sporadic – been difficult to maintain a
relevant and updated case study.

ELIZABETH
I have a family to raise…a job to...

AVERY

So the evaluation is loose at best. Multiple life attempts –
most recently a month ago.

ELIZABETH
She wasn't supposed to come by until Saturday.

AVERY

Her daughter found her while making an early visit
home ...after failing to reach her by phone.

> *(WOMAN 2 (ELIZABETH)'s bathroom. She sits
> on the toilet seat – head in her hands – her
> wrists bandaged up. WOMAN 1 (RACHEL)
> enters in rush. Drops her purse.)*

RACHEL
Shit, Mom. What the hell?

> *(She begins to attend to her Mom.)*
It's everywhere – what were you thinking?

(She is gathering up prescription bottles, a bottle of Jack Daniels and several bloody towels. Elizabeth is clearly intoxicated and coming off some prescription high.)

AVERY
Surrounded by bloody towels and pill bottles.

ELIZABETH
I don't know…wait…those aren't mine.

RACHEL
Come on, Mom…I'm not an…

ELIZABETH
It was just so dark – I couldn't see where I was walking…

RACHEL
Shut up. Mom. I can't be bullshitted today, OK? I have maybe the most important job interview of…

ELIZABETH
Just stay with me...you have to stay with your Mom.

RACHEL
I know you're joking right now, Mom. I've had this scheduled for…

ELIZABETH
I'm your Mom. I had things scheduled once too, and then well I got knocked up, didn't I? Life happens. *(MOM starts to cry...feels bad for the gaslighting guilt trip)* Please…just one more…

RACHEL
It's never just 'one more day,' Mom…don't pull that shit with me.

ELIZABETH

Language!

RACHEL

Really, Mom? *(She holds up a bloody towel)* My cussing is the problem here?

CUE: SHATTERED

They are going to call me any second now. I HAVE to go. I can't miss this.

I KNOW HOW THIS WORKS
I'VE BEEN HERE BEFORE
THE WAR IS BEGUN
I'M BARELY THROUGH THE DOOR
CAN WE CALL THIS A TRUCE?
CAN WE CUT US SOME SLACK?
I'LL GET OFF YOURS
IF YOU GET OFF MY BACK

ELIZABETH

LISTEN, I'M SORRY
YOU KNOW THAT I LOVE YOU
LISTEN, I'M SORRY
BUT YOU HAVE TO KNOW WHAT YOUR WORDS
CAN DO
YOU HAVE TO SEE
WHAT THEY DO TO ME

RACHEL

I DON'T WANT TO FIGHT
LOOK – HERE'S MY WHITE FLAG
I CAN'T DO THIS EVERY TIME I COME HOME
SO OK – THERE – YOU WIN
WON'T DO THIS EVERY TIME I'M HOME
LET'S NOT EVEN BEGIN

RACHEL (CONT)
I WISH IT DIDN'T MATTER
BUT LIKE GLASS - YOU LEAVE ME SHATTERED

LIKE GLASS – YOU LEAVE ME…
LISTEN, I'M SORRY
I KNOW IT'S ALSO MY FAULT

ELIZABETH
LISTEN, I'M SORRY
BUT CAN WE TRY FOR ONCE TO PUT IT AWAY?

BOTH
BURY THE HATCHET
EVEN JUST FOR TODAY
I'LL TRY IF YOU'LL TRY
COME HELL OR HIGH WATER
PUT BACK THE PIECES WE'VE BROKEN
TOGETHER
LIKE MOTHER – LIKE DAUGHTER

>*(RACHEL's phone beeps. She checks it. Gives*
>*up. Decides to stay and forget the interview.*
>*During this final refrain, RACHEL gathers up*
>*pills and alcohol in a bag to take with her.)*

RACHEL
I DON'T WANT TO FIGHT
LOOK – HERE'S MY WHITE FLAG
I CAN'T DO THIS EVERY TIME I COME HOME
SO OK – THERE – YOU WIN
WON'T DO THIS EVERY TIME I'M HOME
LET'S NOT EVEN BEGIN
I WISH IT HADN'T MATTERED
BUT LIKE GLASS - YOU LEAVE ME SHATTERED
SHATTERED
LIKE GLASS – YOU LEAVE ME SHATTERED

*(RACHEL helps ELIZABETH up and out of the
bathroom – sits her down. ELIZABETH grabs
RACHEL'S arm.)*

ELIZABETH

ALL I KNOW TO SAY
IS I'M SORRY FOR THE WAY I DIDN'T KNOW
BETTER
FOR WORSE OR FOR BETTER
I SHOULD'VE KNOWN BETTER

*(RACHEL and ELIZABETH exit as DYLAN
enters holding a folder – his case file.)*

SCENE 4: THE TEXT

*MAN 2 (DYLAN) sits on a couch playing
Assassin's Creed (or whatever current game
makes sense for your production) on his Xbox. It
is clear he has been there for quite a while – a
true gamer. Remnants of food and clothes litter
the area. DYLAN's grabs his phone to send a
text to a romantic interest with whom he has
been on several dates.*

AVERY

Case #8961G. Archival. 2012.

DYLAN

*(tossing his file back to AVERY so as not to
interrupt his video game)*
Name's Dylan.

AVERY

Severe anxiety since childhood.

DYLAN
(Annoyed)

12. I was 12.

AVERY

Most often presenting as extreme OCD, uncontrollable,
 crippling thoughts and compulsions…

DYLAN

One Mississippi…Two Mississippi…Three Mississippi…

> *(continues under dialogue as DYLAN checks the
> door – locks and re-locks it repeatedly- counting
> each time)*

AVERY

Difficulty remaining employed when compulsions are
especially intense. Relationships have been …well…a
challenge.

DYLAN
(Speaking out loud as he texts)
"Hey….what's up..." *(deletes)* "How's your day?"

> *(Now...he just waits. What will be the reply?
> When will it come? What if there's no reply at
> all? He sighs.*

CUE: DON'T BE CRAZY

> *(The spiral of waiting-for-a-reply begins as he
> tries to distract himself with his video game.)*

DYLAN

SO I SENT HER THIS TEXT AT EXACTLY NINE-
THIRTY
I SAID "HEY HOW'S YOUR DAY?" – NOTHING
TOO WORDY
JUST 14 LETTERS LONG, SO WHAT DID I DO
WRONG?
BECAUSE IT'S 10PM AND MY PHONE HASN'T
BEEPED YET
MY MIND'S CREATING STORIES – DON'T KNOW
TO INTERPRET I'M SURE SHE'S AT THE GYM –
FOR SOME YOGA OR A LATE NIGHT SWIM

NO NO NO
I WON'T LET MY MIND CONFUSE ME
NO, NO, NO! I WON'T LET MY HEART DECEIVE
ME
CAN'T ALLOW THIS SCREEN ANYMORE TO PIN
ME TO THE PROVERBIAL FLOOR JUST CALM
AND CHILL – RELAX A BIT
AND DON'T BE CRAZY
NO – DON'T BE CRAZY

One Mississippi, two Mississippi, three Mississippi, four
Mississippi, five…

IT'S 10:15 – I FEEL LIKE SOMETHING IS LURKING
I'D BETTER CALL VERIZON JUST TO CHECK
THAT IT'S WORKING MAYBE SHE TRIED TO
CALL – I NEED TECH SUPPORT, THAT'S ALL OR
MAYBE I SHOULD TAKE A TINY GLANCE AT HER
FACEBOOK OR SNAPCHAT WHILE WE'RE AT IT –
WHAT'S THE HARM IN ONE LOOK? DON'T
WANNA BE A FREAK – JUST TAKE A LITTLE
PEEK

(Bridge...of insanity)

DYLAN (CONT)
BUT WHAT IF SHE'S DONE WITH ME
AND SHE'S IGNORING ME
OR WHAT IF SHE MET A MAN
STARTED MAKING PLANS?
AND BY 11:15 I'LL BE ALONE
FOREVER AND EVER BE ALONE
JUST ME, MY CAT, AND MY iPHONE
DRUNKEN, JOBLESS, STUCK AT HOME
WE ALL KNOW WHAT HAPPENS NEXT
ALL BECAUSE I SENT THAT TEXT!

> *(Calms himself down. Tries to circumvent the "crazy")*

I mean that's one possible option.

> SO TIME IS TICKING BY AND TENSION IS
> MOUNTING
> 57 MINUTES, 30 SECONDS – BUT WHO'S
> COUNTING?
> I NEED A XANAX STAT – IS THERE AN APP FOR
> THAT?
> SO NETFLIX IS IN ORDER – NEED A REAL
> DISTRACTION
> DESPERATE MEASURES OFTEN CALL FOR
> DESPERATE ACTION
> NOT SURE HOW THIS ENDS – AND LOOK IT'S
> SEASON ONE OF "FRIENDS"

> *(Music stops, DYLAN is entranced, even emotional)*

(Spoken) Joey is just SOO misunderstood…AHHH!

> *(and suddenly he throws the remote – he has even scared himself.)*

DYLAN (CONT)

NO NO NO
I WON'T LET MY MIND CONFUSE ME
NO, NO, NO! I WON'T LET MY HEART DECEIVE ME
CALM AND CHILL – RELAX A BIT
AND DON'T BE … *(breathing, nearly like Lamaze)*
AND DON'T BE… *(calming himself..)*
DON'T BE…

> *(Phone beeps. He scrambles to answer it, knocking over anything in his way. Once in his hands he carefully and cautiously opens the text screen as if it were a suspicious package that could explode at any moment.)*

DYLAN
(reading aloud)

"Hey."

> *(pause – sudden relief. Melts into couch exhausted. Music begins again.)*

Whew. That was close.

> *(Button. Beat. Lights shift to AVERY in her apartment and MACY at home in her childhood bedroom. They are Facetiming.)*

SCENE 5: BLANKET FORTS AND FLASHLIGHTS

AVERY
You can't just let him talk to you that way.

MACY
It's just Zach being Zach. He's stressed and busy. I get it. So am I...I have three days to get…

AVERY
(overlapping)
That doesn't matter and it's not an excuse.

MACY
…this client's website finished and uploaded and then there are three more I haven't even started yet…

AVERY
You need to break up with him…

MACY
(exploding)
You don't know *what* I need!!

(long beat)

MACY
I'm sorry…I just...Between my boss hounding me…..and I don't want to trigger an episode...it's just...a lot.

AVERY
(overlapping)
No…I'm sorry… You're right, I shouldn't assume things about you or what you're…ya know.

MACY
…and picking up new clients is good but trying to keep up just has me a little crazed.

AVERY
…plus with Mom just...not...there.

MACY
I know.

(Beat.)

CUE: BACK THEN

MACY
I miss you. *(Too much?)* I mean...this. I miss...this.

AVERY
Is everything else okay?

MACY
Just need you.

AVERY
(Out on a limb - 'cause why not?)
Come up this weekend.

MACY
And stay in the bathtub?

AVERY
We can share the twin – like old times.

MACY
But you're busy and you have all your work to do…

AVERY
Macy…

MACY
…and I've got all *my* work to finish before Saturday…

AVERY
Macy…

MACY
(really wanting to say yes)
Okay yes…I'll be there Friday…

AVERY

Good…bring your work.

(beat)

MACY

Things were easier when we both lived at home.

AVERY

Yeah – weirdly, yeah. They were.

(As lyric begins, Facetime shifts to real time – and we see them live – many miles apart)

MACY

YOU AND I IN PJ'S
WHISPERING ALL NIGHT
PLANNING FUTURES TOGETHER
BY A FADING FLASHLIGHT
I'D GIVE ANYTHING FOR ANOTHER DAY
LIKE THE ONES WE HAD BACK THEN

AVERY

We were so ridiculous, weren't we?

MACY

We weren't jaded yet. That's all.

OUR WORLD WAS A GIANT FORT OF BLANKETS
PLAYING TRUTH OR DARE
NO TOPIC WAS OFF LIMITS
NO WORDS WE COULDN'T SHARE
WHAT I'D GIVE TO BE THAT WAY AGAIN
LIKE THE WAY WE WERE BACK THEN

AVERY
BUT LIFE GOT IN THE WAY
AS THE NIGHT TURNED INTO DAY
AND THE WAY WE WERE BECAME THE WAY WE
ARE

     (beat)
I NEVER MEANT TO DRIFT SO FAR

MACY
I know. But I understand. *(beat)* So maybe this weekend we can remedy this...*I* can remedy...this thing that happened that ...ya know...

AVERY
Flashlights, blankets?

MACY
Yeah.

AVERY AND MACY
THE WAY WE WERE BACK THEN
THE WAY WE WERE
THE WAY YOU AND I WERE BACK THEN

AVERY
Friday?

MACY
Peasy.

AVERY
Peasy.

     (Button.)

SCENE 6: HOW IT FEELS

AVERY

Case number...

LAURA
(interrupting)
6731K. Ongoing. And it's Laura – don't even bother –
nothing helps.

AVERY

Aggression brought on by bouts of depression rooted in
Cluster A Paranoid Personality Disorder with early signs of
mild schizophrenia - namely, auditory hallucinations.
Antipsychotic for 9 months. Primary symptoms include
extreme mistrust of others, hypersensitivity; perceived
attacks from known and unknown forces. Her boyfriend,
Charlie has asked her to move in with him. She is resisting.

> *(LAURA sits center stage on a park bench with*
> *CHARLIE. They are mid-conversation. The*
> *ensemble serves as the voices in LAURA's head.)*

CHARLIE

I AM trying, Laura. I know you may think I'm not. I just
don't understand...I thought this was the obvious next step
for us.

LAURA

That's my whole point. NO ONE understands. Not even me.

ENSEMBLE AND CHARLIE

Then explain it to me again.

LAURA

It's not just something you 'get over' or forget about.

(WOMAN 1 appears isolated at another part of the stage)

WOMAN 1

When I get depressed, I just get over it

CHARLIE

So – when does it happen? Does something trigger you feeling this way?

(MAN 1 appears isolated at another part of the stage)

MAN 1

You just need to stop feeling sorry for yourself, if you ask me.

LAURA

No. That would be so much easier – I never know when I'll have an …attack. It's like an attack.

CHARLIE

And who …or what is attacking you?

(WOMAN 2 and MAN 2 appear isolated at another part of the stage)

WOMAN 2

You don't LOOK sick – you just need to exercise.

MAN 2

You're not trying hard enough.

LAURA

I don't know…I just don't know.

CHARLIE

What can I do? Is there something I can do?

WOMAN 1

Stop being selfish.

MAN 1

You just want attention.

LAURA

No.

WOMAN 2

You have a loving family – I don't understand what you have to be anxious or depressed about.

MAN 2

Are you praying? Maybe you aren't trusting God enough.

CHARLIE

Maybe we should start over. From the beginning. Can you tell me exactly how it feels? In YOUR words...

CUE: THREE DAYS WITHOUT BREATHING

WOMAN 1

It's all in your mind.

MAN 1

Medication will make it worse.

LAURA

I can try.

WOMAN 2

You're just lazy.

MAN 2

Stop wasting his time.

LAURA

YOU ASK ME HOW IT FEELS
AND I DON'T KNOW HOW TO SAY IT
YOU ASK ABOUT THE HEAVINESS
I DON'T KNOW HOW TO WEIGH IT
YOU ASK WHY I CAN'T JUST STOP
AND QUIET THE LITTLE VOICE
YOU ASK WHY I LET IT TAKE OVER
AND YOU THINK I HAVE A CHOICE

CHARLIE

It's not like that…I just…

LAURA

Charlie – just let me finish, OK?

SO HERE – HERE'S THE BEST I CAN DO
THE WAY IT FEELS…
IMAGINE THREE DAYS WITHOUT BREATHING
THREE DAYS NOT INHALING
FAILING TO TAKE IN THE AIR
IMAGINE THREE DAYS WITHOUT BREATHING
AND YOU'LL ALMOST BE THERE

*(The 'voices' descend on her during this next
section in an almost choreographed assault –
Laura is aware of them, but Charlie is not)*

MAN 1

Are you kidding yourself right now?

WOMAN 2

It's time to face reality.

MAN 2

He's humoring you - you know that right? He doesn't
actually believe you.

WOMAN 3

NO one believes you.

LAURA ENSEMBLE

IT'S LIKE BEING ATTACKED OOH. OOH. FROM
THE INSIDE OUT
BOXING WITH YOUR BRAIN
AND NEVER WINNING THE BOUT
TEXTING EVERYONE YOU KNOW
AND FEELING LIKE A CREEP LIKE A CREEP
DRINKING IT ALL AWAY AT NIGHT ALL AWAY
JUST TO GET A LITTLE SLEEP

(She returns to CHARLIE – the voices vanish)

BUT WITH YOU
WITH YOU I'M CALMER
YES WITH YOU
WITH YOU I'M CALMER
I'M SORRY I CAN'T BE BETTER YET
BUT IN CASE IT HELPS TO KNOW

HERE'S THE BEST I CAN DO…

IMAGINE THREE DAYS WITHOUT BREATHING
THREE DAYS NOT INHALING
FAILING TO TAKE IN THE AIR
IMAGINE THREE DAYS WITHOUT BREATHING
THREE DAYS AND YOU'LL ALMOST BE THERE
WITHOUT BREATHING

(CHARLIE goes to speak. LAURA stops him.)

LAURA (CONT)
JUST GIVE ME THREE DAYS THREE DAYS
WITHOUT BREATHING
AND I'LL ALMOST BE THERE

> *(LAURA starts to exit. CHARLIE stands up as if to go after her. Calls to her.)*

CHARLIE

Laura.

> *(She stops. Does not turn around.)*

I see you.

LAURA

Don't say that just 'cause you think I need to …

CHARLIE
> *(interrupting)*

I see you. I hear you.

> *(LAURA turns around. CHARLIE walks to her, keeping his eyes focused directly on her - maybe for the first time. After a beat, LAURA throws her arms around CHARLIE to his surprise. He sighs.)*

SCENE 7: THE END OF THINGS

> *(ANNIE makes her way across the room and sets the box down.)*

AVERY

CASE #7108H. Archival. 2006.

ANNIE

(Distracted. Hands file to AVERY from a box of belongings through which she is rummaging for something she cannot seem to find.)

Annie.

AVERY

Depression. Severe. Several clinicians suggest Bipolar as the manic stages keep patient awake for as many as three days at a time.

ANNIE

Where the hell are they?

AVERY

Manifests in fits of rage, paranoia, and delusion.

ANNIE

There.

(relieved – she pulls out her house key from the box)

AVERY

Her marriage of ten years has dissolved.

(MAN 1 (NEIL) stands in the kitchen facing out the window in silence. After a few moments, WOMAN 2 (ANNIE) enters and stops cold. The tension is palpable.)

ANNIE

So…just leave the key here or…

NEIL

Fine.

(beat)

ANNIE

And uh…I left the books in the bedroom – I didn't know where you…

NEIL
(interrupting)

OK.

(beat)

ANNIE

OK- so…well I guess I'm gonna go…

(She waits for a response. Gets none. Turns to leave. She stops herself.)

NEIL

So what could I have done differently, exactly?

ANNIE

Neil, we've been through all of this…

NEIL

No, I mean it. What else could I have possibly done? I was there for it all, wasn't I?

ANNIE

Yes – it wasn't about…

NEIL

The therapy? The attacks? The mania? These...pills??

ANNIE

Neil…

NEIL

…and all the vomiting? The endless vomiting. You can't just take them whenever you feel like it.

ANNIE

I said I was sorry.

NEIL

I never asked for 'sorry,' Annie.

(beat)

ANNIE

It's just something I have to do alone…at least for…

NEIL

NOW? – Suddenly NOW you have to do it alone?

ANNIE

I know how late this is…

NEIL

Late, Annie? Late?? 10 years – 10 years of this…

ANNIE

(appealing - pleading for the love they shared)
Were they really *all* a waste? We built a life here - on that porch…in that living room…and...

> *(Beat. NEIL is silent – turns away from her. He has said his peace.)*

CUE: SHOULD'VE KNOWN BETTER

ANNIE

I'VE ALWAYS LOVED THIS KITCHEN
EVEN THOUGH I'M A TERRIBLE COOK
YOU KNOW I'M A TERRIBLE COOK
BUT I LOVE BEING IN THIS ROOM
BEING WITH YOU IN THIS ROOM
PLEASE SAY SOMETHING – ANYTHING
DON'T JUST LOOK AT ME THAT WAY
WITH NOTHING TO SAY

I COULD SAY THIS HURTS FOR ME AS MUCH AS
YOU
I COULD SAY I KNOW EXACTLY WHAT YOU'RE
GOING THROUGH I COULD SAY I SYMPATHIZE
WITH THE TEARS IN YOUR EYES

NEIL

BUT WE BOTH KNOW BETTER

ANNIE

I COULD SAY THE PAIN WON'T CUT STRAIGHT
TO THE BONE
I COULD SAY YOU'LL SEE YOU'RE BETTER OFF
ALONE
I COULD SAY YOUR ANGER NOW WILL FADE
AWAY SOMEHOW

NEIL

BUT WE BOTH KNOW BETTER
HARD TO SAY WHAT I FEEL RIGHT NOW
HARD TO STAND HERE AND AT LAST HEAR THE
TRUTH

*(NEIL tries to exit the room – ANNIE grabs him
at the peak of desperation)*

ANNIE

BUT I LOVED YOU EVERY DAY
I KNOW YOU DON'T BELIEVE IT

NEIL

YOU CAN'T EXPECT ME TO BELIEVE IT
CAUSE I LOVED YOU EVERY WAY

BOTH

AND WHERE WE STAND DEPENDS ON HOW THIS
ENDS

NEIL

I COULD SAY I WILL UNDERSTAND THIS AND
FORGET

ANNIE

I COULD SAY WE WON'T BE HAUNTED BY
REGRET
I COULD SAY THAT TIME WILL HEAL THE WAY
I'VE MADE YOU FEEL BUT WE BOTH KNOW
BETTER

NEIL

WE BOTH KNOW BETTER

NEIL

Let's not forget - YOU are leaving ME, remember?

(NEIL exits. ANNIE continues...alone)

ANNIE

SO ALL I KNOW TO SAY
IS I'M SORRY FOR THE WAY
I DIDN'T KNOW BETTER
FOR WORSE OR FOR BETTER
I SHOULD'VE KNOWN BETTER

(ANNIE takes one box to the door. She exits.)

SCENE 8: SO MUCH TO SAY

(AVERY speaks. DAN hands her his file.)

AVERY

Case number 5601G. Ongoing.

DAN

Daniel…or Dan. Whatever.

AVERY

Generalized Anxiety with lengthy bouts of depression that bear resemblance to Adjustment Disorder rooted in parental abandonment. Physical abandonment at age 8 by his father.

DAN

He went to put gas in the Volvo.

AVERY

Emotional abandonment by mother thereafter.

DAN

She just shut down…completely.

AVERY

Therapy has proven effective and lasting. Been off anxiety medication for some time.

DAN

They made me nauseous – I was happy to stop.

AVERY

Demonstrating progress particularly in terms of social anxiety.

DAN

Things were going so well.

AVERY

Sudden sharp decline instigated by return of primary trigger.

DAN

Just knocked on my door…out the blue.

> *(DAN stares in disbelief at his father – on his doorstep – 15 years since he was abandoned)*

DAN

What are you…..why are you here?

CUE: SOMETHING LIKE LOVE

DAN'S FATHER
SO THERE'S SO MUCH TO SAY
I MEAN I GUESS THERE IS
ITS LIKE YEARS OF WORDS READY TO BURST
THAT SUDDENLY WON'T COME
BUT HERE I AM STANDING
HERE I AM STANDING
I GUESS BETTER LATE THAN NEVER

I WANT TO SAY I'M SORRY
AND ASK IF YOU'RE OK
BEEN SITTING IN MY CAR OUT BACK
REHEARSING THIS ALL DAY
BUT THE TRUTH IS WHEN IT COMES TO YOU
I'VE NEVER FOUND THE WORDS
ALL I KNEW – WHEN I LOOKED AT YOU
WAS SOMETHING LIKE LOVE

SO I'M HERE NOW IN YOUR DOORWAY
AND I KNOW YOU WONDER HOW

DAN'S FATHER (CONT)
IF THERE'S ANYTHING YOU WANT FROM ME
I GUESS THE TIME IS NOW
THE TRUTH IS I HAVE ALWAYS LOVED YOU
AND ALWAYS WILL SOMEHOW

I'm sorry I didn't tell you before…but now that we're face to
 face…

DAN
ONE MISSISSIPPI
TWO MISSISSIPPI
THREE MISSISSIPPI
FOUR MISSISSIPPI
FIVE

DAN'S FATHER
Did you get my letters?

CUE: HERE ON MY OWN

DAN
Letters? Yeah..I got your letters.

'I'M SORRY' WAS WHAT IT SAID
'I WAS SCARED' IS WHAT I READ
SEVEN LETTERS TO END ALL THE THINGS THAT
WE SHARED 'I'M SORRY' - ALL IT SAID
'I WAS SCARED' IS WHAT I READ
AND THAT WAS IT

Finished. Over. Done.

AN ENDING I COULDN'T REPAIR
BUT THE END OF US DIDN'T MEAN THE END OF
ME

DAN (CONT)
Do you have any idea what happened to
us? To Mom? To me?

DAN'S FATHER
I was not in a good place...I needed to take care of...

DAN
I THOUGHT IT WAS HOPELESS – I THOUGHT
THAT I BLEW IT THE WORLD I HAD KNOWN WAS
GONE AS I KNEW IT BUT I'M STRONGER THAN
THAT
AND I HAVE SURVIVED ON MY OWN
I THOUGHT I WAS DYING AND LIVED LIFE
REGRETTING THE SUN IN MY SKY HAD FADED
TO SETTING
BUT YOU CAN'T HAVE THAT
I'VE MADE IT JUST FINE ON MY OWN
ON MY OWN

SO LIVE YOUR LIFE LIKE I NEVER EVEN
MATTERED
I CAN'T WAKE EACH DAY WONDERING HOW
IT'S MY FAULT I'M ALONE LIVE YOUR LIFE LIKE
MY WORLD NEVER SHATTERED 'CAUSE YOU
WEREN'T THERE
AND I DON'T CARE
I'M BETTER I SWEAR ON MY OWN

I was 8 years old. Who does that to an 8 year old??

DAN'S FATHER
(defensive)
Hey - I was doing the best I could! The best I knew how….

DAN
I THOUGHT I WOULD HARBOR A SEA OF
RESENTMENT WHEN ONE MAN DESTROYS ALL I
ONCE CALLED CONTENTMENT BUT THAT WAS
BEFORE I KNEW I WAS FINE ON MY OWN I
THOUGHT I COULD DRINK ALL THE HURT LEFT
BEHIND TRIED TO FORGET ALL THE 'YOU'
CLOGGING UP MY MIND BUT I KNOW THAT
NOW
I'VE FOUND MYSELF HERE ON MY OWN - ON
MY OWN SO – LIVE YOU LIFE LIKE MY WORLD
NEVER STOPPED TURNING THAT EIGHT YEAR
OLD KID'S NOW A MAN YOU DON'T KNOW LIVE
YOU LIFE AS IF MINE WERE NOT BURNING
'CAUSE YOU WEREN'T THERE
AND I DON'T EVEN CARE
I'M BETTER, I SWEAR, ON MY OWN

DAN'S FATHER
ALL I KNOW TO SAY IS I'M SORRY FOR THE WAY

DAN
YOU SHOULD'VE KNOWN BETTER

I think it's time you leave…

(DAN waits for him to go)
SO I'LL GO ON WITH A NEW STRENGTH
DISCOVERED
THE ME I FOUND ON THE BACKSIDE OF SHAME
SO LIVE YOUR LIFE AND I WILL LIVE MINE
UNAFRAID OF MYSELF
MY HEART OFF THE SHELF AND MY OWN
SO THANK YOU FOR ALL THE PAIN
I'M PROUD OF WHAT HAS REMAINED
FINALLY BETTER OFF HERE ON MY OWN

(Blackout)

SCENE 9 - NO-SHOW

CUE: MACY DOESN'T SHOW

> *(Friday. Split stage. On one side, MACY sits at a bar alone. She is clearly three-quarters of her way through a drinking binge. On the other side, AVERY sits at a campus coffee shop - the agreed-upon meeting time and place for the planned "sister weekend." AVERY can be texting [or using an app like Snapchat] to send messages. This can be projected, spoken or any combination thereof. We hear MACY's incoming message alert each time. The ensemble stands observing.)*

AVERY
I'm here. We did say 9, yes?

> *(beat)*

AVERY
Hurry. I'm being stared down by a creeper. LOL.

> *(beat. MACY checks her phone. Sets it back down. Another beat.)*

AVERY
Hello???!!

> *(Beat. MACY checks phone again. Sets it down again.)*

MACY
(to bartender)
Yeah - one more…

BARTENDER
You sure? Been at it pretty heavy all week.

MACY
Relationships suck - am I right?

BARTENDER
(handing her a drink)
This one's on me.

ENSEMBLE
I COULD BE YOUR HERE NOW

(Coffee shop lights start to slowly be turned off one by one. They are closing.)

AVERY
Where are you? Did something happen?

ENSEMBLE
I COULD BE YOUR LONG GONE

(AVERY wastes no time. She calls MACY, whose phone rings. She grabs her phone. She is going to answer….beat….she turns ringer off instead. She is reluctant but too ashamed to answer. AVERY, feeling the pressure, begins to exit - makes one more effort.)

AVERY
Macy, what the hell? Coffee shop is closed - just come to the apartment.

(she hits send, walks outside.)

ENSEMBLE
I COULD BE YOUR DETOUR
I COULD BE YOUR STREET SIGN

AVERY
At least call...a text...SOMETHING...I'm legitimately
worried now.

ENSEMBLE
I COULD BE THE ONE WHO ALWAYS STAYED
STAYED
STAYED

MACY
(Checks phone. Does not answer.)
(to herself) Can't make it, Ave. Sorry.

CUE: LAST CALL

*(Lights dark on AVERY. MACY nurses her last
drink.)*
IT'S BAD ENOUGH I'M IN THIS MESS
WITHOUT DRAGGING PEOPLE DOWN
BOTH ME AND VODKA ON THE ROCKS
IN A LONELY LITTLE TOWN
NO ONE TO HURT IF I STAY AWAY
AND AVOID THE WHEEL OF MY CHEVROLET
KEEP THE FEAR AT BAY
FOR ANOTHER DAY

THE JUKEBOX PLAYS ANOTHER SONG
RELENTLESS WORDS 'BOUT "DONE ME
WRONG"
AND THE BARTENDER SINGS ALONG
AND POURS ME ANOTHER DRINK...I THINK

MACY (CONT)

I HEAR HIM SAY "LAST CALL" AND I START
SHAKING
WHAT WILL I DO WHEN I HAVE TO LEAVE?
I HAVE NOWHERE TO GO – AND NO WAY TO
SLOW THE SPEEDING TRAIN INSIDE MY BRAIN
FEELING SMALL – LAST CALL – AND WHEN SHE
CALLED I SAID NO
WHY DID I SAY NO?
WHAT IF THAT WAS THE LAST CALL?

MAYBE IF I HIDE THE MESS I AM
I CAN WORK IT OUT ON MY OWN
BUT MIDNIGHT'S CREEPING IN AGAIN
LIKE A GAUNTLET BEING THROWN
ALICIA KEYS SINGS FROM THE JUKEBOX CHOIR
TELLING ME ALL ABOUT A 'GIRL ON FIRE'
AND I WONDER IF IT'S ME
AND IF MY FLAMES ARE BRIGHT ENOUGH TO
SEE

I HEAR HIM SAY "LAST CALL" AND I START
FREAKING
WHAT WILL I DO WHEN I HAVE TO LEAVE
I HAVE NO ONE TO CALL – AND I FEEL THE FALL
– THE RACING THOUGHT THAT I'M ALL BUT
CAUGHT
IN THIS CRAWL – LAST CALL – BUT THEN AVERY
CALLED
AND I SAID NO
WHY DID I SAY NO
OH GOD - DON'T LET THAT BE THE LAST CALL
BOTH ME AND VODKA ON THE ROCKS
AND THE TIME IN ENDLESS TICKS AND TOCKS
THE TEARS WON'T FALL - FINALLY HIT THE
WALL
THIS IS IT - THIS IS DONE - THAT IS ALL

MACY (CONT

THE LAST CALL
THE LAST CALL

(blackout)

***NOTE - Should you choose an act break, this is where it
should happen. Please use the latter half of "Last Call"
instrumentally as an Entr'acte of sorts.**

AVERY
*(Frustrated. Answers are not coming as quickly as she would
like.)*
Mental illness *should* be like any other illness, right? You
get sick, you get treated, you get well. The problem is - well
I don't know what the problem is. THAT'S the problem. It's
just too subjective right now - and medicine can't be
subjective - it just can't. I can't do my job if I'm just
guessing based on some random questionnaire.

SCENE 10– AWKWARD

AVERY
Case number 5308H. Ongoing.

CARA

*(steps out for what is clearly a much needed
smoke break. CARA often uses humor at
inappropriate times. This is her defensive
mechanism to combat the otherwise serious
nature of her situation.)*
Cara.

AVERY
Recovering Alcoholic. Nearing completion of 12 steps.

CARA
Number 9, in fact.

AVERY
Self-medicated this way for 10 years to handle clinical depression and manic behaviors. Having trouble reconciling her past actions – especially while intoxicated. Several DUI violations. The last of which resulted in an injury-related accident leaving patient with non-life threatening injuries. Once released, Cara just disappeared for a while – cutting off all ties.

CARA
I had to figure things out, OK? Don't judge.

AVERY
Cara's step 9 involves, among others, a former friend.

JOE
We were actually sort of a thing…I guess?

CARA
(Implying they were intimate at the very least)
We were *definitely* a thing. Joe and I haven't spoken since. Not once.

AVERY
High risk of relapse as she re-enters her former social circle.

(CARA approaches JOE. They clearly have a past – and haven't seen each other in years.)

CUE: SO ANYWAY

CARA
(Immediately putting out cigarette)
Oh my gosh…How are you?

JOE

I'm good…wow – How are you? It's been what….6 or 7…

CARA

A long time.

JOE

Yeah.

CARA

Yeah.

SO I DIDN'T KNOW I'D RUN INTO YOU TONIGHT
I JUST CAME TO SUPPORT A FRIEND
SHE'S THE REDHEAD OVER THERE
YEAH
SO ANYWAY

JOE

YOU LOOK GOOD – LIKE MAYBE YOU'VE LOST
WEIGHT
OR SOMETHING NEW ABOUT YOUR HAIR OR
MAYBE…
WELL IT'S BEEN AWHILE
SO ANYWAY

CARA

ARE YOU STILL WRITING SONGS? CAUSE I'VE
STOPPED WRITING SONGS DIDN'T SEE THE
POINT – IT WASN'T LEADING ANYWHERE
BUT YOU – YOU WERE GOOD

JOE

Stop…

CARA
NO I MEAN YOU WERE GREAT – I LOVED THAT
ONE ABOUT YOUR MOM AND DAD

(beat – JOE has nothing to say)

SO ANYWAY…
I WAS REALLY SORRY TO HEAR ABOUT YOUR
DAD

BOTH
I WOULD'VE CALLED BUT WASN'T SURE IF…

CARA
WELL…

JOE
YOU KNOW…

CARA
AND CONSIDERING THE CIRCUMSTANCES
SO ANYWAY
REMEMBER WHEN WE ALL WENT SKIING
I WAS DRUNK
WELL WE ALL WERE
AND YOUR DAD COULDN'T STOP LAUGHING
AND YOU AND I – WE SANG THE NIGHT AWAY AT
KARAOKE

BOTH
"BOHEMIAN RHAPSODY" NEVER SOUNDED SO
BAD

CARA
WE WERE HAPPY, FREEZING AND…

JOE

DRINKING…..

Let's not forget that.

    (beat)

CARA

SO ANYWAY

    (beat)
I DIDN'T KNOW I'D RUN INTO YOU TONIGHT
I JUST CAME TO SUPPORT A FRIEND
AND I'D PROBABLY BETTER GET BACK IN
THERE
SO ANYWAY…
IT WAS GOOD TO SEE YOU

JOE

Yeah…you too.

    *(CARA turns to leave. This was way harder than
    she had imagined. She turns back.)*

CARA

I'm in a program.

JOE

Oh yeah? Good.

CARA

Third time's the charm.

JOE

Well let's hope…

CARA

AND BY THE WAY – I DON'T BLAME YOU FOR ANYTHING

JOE

AND I'M NOT MAD AT YOU ANYMORE

(beat – CARA is clearly relieved)

SO ANYWAY…

JOE

SO YEAH…

CARA

SO ANYWAY…

(Awkward 'do we hug or do we shake hands' goodbye. So they do something awkwardly in-between. They both exit.)

SCENE 11: SUCH DEVOTED SISTERS

(MACY is waiting impatiently at Starbucks – nursing a coffee. After a few seconds, AVERY runs in overloaded with bags and laptop and the accouterments of a student at their wit's end.)

AVERY

I'm sorry..I'm sorry. My Advanced Psych Prof literally never shuts up – ironic for a course all about listening –

MACY

It's fine.

(hands her a coffee – which she already purchased for her)

AVERY

Oh thanks…is it…?

MACY

Double shot.

AVERY

And did you add…?

MACY

Skim.

AVERY

Awesome *(takes a sip)*. What do I owe you?

MACY
(without missing a beat)

100 dollars

AVERY
(also quick to the punch)

How about 5?

(hands her a $5 bill)

MACY

Keep it.

(beat)

AVERY

What happened the other night?

MACY
(simple as if it was no big deal)
I'm sorry.

AVERY
I called...sent a million messages…

MACY
(Defensive)
Bad night. Why do you care?

AVERY
Are you kidding?...I was worried sick about it...you can't just vanish whenever you...

MACY
I said I was sorry.

(beat)

AVERY
You should really go back to school…

MACY
No...that's not what we're gonna do today.

AVERY
Why not? It would be good for you and all this...stuff...that you…

MACY
Stuff? What stuff? My unique brand of crazy?

AVERY
I didn't say …

MACY

You didn't have to.

(beat)

AVERY

I moved. I left. It made a world of difference for me just getting...

MACY

Well – we aren't all as fucking smart as you…

AVERY

Macy, come on…

MACY

…or Dad's favorite…

AVERY

That's not fair and…

MACY
(more cutting than she actually intends)
And it's not as easy when you're the alcoholic family fuck-up with a princess sister who shits golden eggs….see, that's kinda hard to compete with.

(long beat)

MACY

I'm sorry.

AVERY

No – it's fine..I…

MACY

That's not how I meant…

AVERY

I know…

MACY

It's just....*(very long beat)* …can I stay with you?

AVERY

Oh Mace, I don't…

MACY

Just for a little while. I have a job – I can help pay.

AVERY

It's not the money…I have literally one room – one bed..and after Friday...I just need...

MACY
(Takes her time)
Mom's worse lately. She just sits there. Like she's here but not. I never see her eat. She doesn't go out. She's...an abandoned house, Ave. A shell. I can't live there anymore. Maybe that makes me a terrible daughter or whatever but…

AVERY

It doesn't.

MACY
(Just realizing this and maybe saying it out loud for the first time)
... I can't...help her. *(beat)* Just 'till I get my head in order?

(another beat)
A few days even.

(beat)

AVERY

Can I think about it?

MACY
(frustrated; subtext: I should never have asked)
Of course…yes…of course.

AVERY

Ok.

(beat...then MACY leaves)

AVERY

I don't shit golden eggs by the way…

(becomes aware she just said that in a room full of Starbucks customers)

SCENE 12: LASAGNA AND BRUISES

AVERY

I realize more and more that all of this data is only based on those who actually SEEK help. What about those who don't? I'm afraid that all of this *(refers to the files)* is just the part of the iceberg I can see. It's the ones UNDER the water that scare me the most.

(beat)
Case number 8611T. Ongoing.

(ETHAN enters - file in hand)

ETHAN

(handing AVERY his file)
Ethan.

AVERY
Often stays indoors for weeks at a time. Presents with
symptoms most closely linked to Borderline Personality
Disorder.

ETHAN
Translation: I'm crazy *and* a recluse.

AVERY
Self-deprecation is a defense mechanism. As is violence.
The bipolar is often manifesting in violent outbursts – many
of which he has no recollection of.

ETHAN
I hit her once. *(as if that makes it okay)*

AVERY
Six reported cases against his girlfriend, Molly.

ETHAN
And that one was an accident.

AVERY
Four of which required immediate medical attention.

ETHAN
It's not like she went to the hospital or anything. We got in a
little spat.

AVERY
His medication seems to have dropped off and become
ineffective.

ETHAN

She got in a couple of good swings too, ya know!

AVERY

So he has stopped taking it. Needs re-evaluated.

ETHAN

She forgave me. It..was fine. I told her it would never happen again.

> *(An apartment. ETHAN and MOLLY stand across a room from each other. MOLLY'S FRIEND stands silently near door with MOLLY's luggage. She is helping MOLLY should her final departure escalate. ETHAN stands with a coffee cup in his hand. MOLLY reacts early in this scene in fear of ETHAN until she builds her confidence - a sort of partner-abuse PTSD.)*

ETHAN

Have everything?

MOLLY

I think so.

ETHAN

Let me carry that down…

MOLLY

No. I'm fine. You don't need to…

ETHAN

Just let me do it!

MOLLY

No. We're fine. It's….fine.

ETHAN

I love you.

MOLLY

Don't make it harder, Ethan.

ETHAN

But I do.

MOLLY

Here's the key. And … thank you.

ETHAN

Thank you? We weren't roommates, ya know…I wasn't exactly your landlord.

MOLLY
(Explosive)

Well I WAS the one paying rent.
(thinks better of that comment)
I know…I'm sorry…this might not be forever.

ETHAN

Feels like it…

MOLLY

You just need time. And help.

ETHAN

I have YOU to help me. No one else knows…

MOLLY

No I can't do it.

ETHAN

Yes you can – if you wanted to *(gaslighting at full gas)*

(MOLLY'S FRIEND steps forward - on alert.
MOLLY motions to her - she's got this.)

MOLLY

You think I haven't tried? Cleaning up your mess?
Wondering which "Ethan" I get today? On the luckier days, I
get to have a pleasant breakfast before you start hurling shit
at me. But most days, I pray that I get out of the house
before you wake up. And hell – that would be easy, right? I
would have left a long time ago – but then I come home to
find roses and movie nights and love notes and lasagna.

CUE: DODGING BULLETS

I can't do it anymore. I want to – but I can't. I can't bounce
between lasagna and bruises anymore, Ethan. You're not
healthy. And neither am I.

ETHAN

Molly, please...you can't just...up and walk away–

I'M NOT WALKING AWAY FROM YOU
I'M WALKING TOWARD MYSELF
NOT RIPPING UP OUR PHOTOS - JUST TAKING
THEM OFF THE SHELF
I WILL NOT TIP-TOE THROUGH YOUR LAND
MINES
ONLY TO FIND THIS TIME
IT'S ME YOU'RE GUNNING FOR
TO SETTLE SOME INVISIBLE SCORE
WELL NOT ANYMORE

YOU PUSH THEN YOU PULL IT'S
LIKE DODGING BULLETS WITH YOU
I'M EMPTY - YOU'RE FULL IT'S
LIKE DODGING BULLETS AROUND YOU
INTENDED OR NOT - YOU HAVE A KNACK

ETHAN (CONT)

FOR MAKING ME FEEL I'VE A TARGET ON MY
BACK
AND DESPITE MY FORGIVENESS, INSISTENCE,
RESISTANCE
I REFUSE TO STAY WITHIN STRIKING DISTANCE
WAITING AROUND FOR ROUND TWO
DODGING BULLETS FROM YOU

ETHAN

I get it. I'm sorry I couldn't…or didn't…

MOLLY

No…you did mostly what you could…*(she grabs his pills)*…
but these, Ethan. They don't work if you don't take them.

ETHAN

They make me jittery…

MOLLY

(Finally fully standing up for herself)
I can't go to the hospital again because you don't want to
feel 'jittery'!

MOLLY AND MOLLY'S FRIEND

*(MOLLY'S FRIEND eventually stops singing as
she feels MOLLY is confident)*
I AM WORTHY
I KNOW I'M WORTHY
I DON'T WANT TO FEEL THE SHAME OR TAKE
THE BLAME

MOLLY
I WILL NOT TIP-TOE THROUGH YOUR LAND
MINES
ONLY TO FIND THIS TIME
IT'S ME YOU'RE GUNNING FOR
TO SETTLE SOME INVISIBLE SCORE
WELL NOT ANYMORE
NO MORE DODGING BULLETS WITH YOU

ETHAN
I'm sorry.

MOLLY
I know you are.

(She turns to leave. He stops her.)

ETHAN
You'll call?

MOLLY
(her tone begins to soften a bit)
Of course.

ETHAN
And it's okay if I…

MOLLY
Of course...yes.

ETHAN
...Just to make sure you're…ya know.

MOLLY
Okay.

(She turns again to go. MOLLY'S FRIEND exits.)

ETHAN

There's…so much to say.

MOLLY

(Stopping at the door. Not angry but rather almost begging)
Then for God's sake – say it.

(Silence. Long beat. He doesn't know what to say. MOLLY turns to leave. ETHAN starts to stop her – but what's the point, now? She's already gone.)

SCENE 13 : 8th PERIOD

AVERY

(Filing through a large number of files - all in the same folder)
Case numbers…

VARIOUS LINCOLN HIGH SCHOOL STUDENTS

(Facing audience and announcing their numbers overlapping until it is almost unintelligible. Subtext : There are so many of them!)

7821L
4328R
4509B
3216T
9021H
8743G
4119K

(Etc, etc – the numbers fade to a whisper and repeat but do not go away as AVERY speaks again. NOTE – be sure the numbers (A) Follow the same 4-number-1-letter sequence and (B) do not use any of the previous case numbers in the show.)

AVERY

All between the ages of 14 and 18 – all witnesses to...well...survivors of... a mass shooting at their high school – all showing clear signs of PTSD – mass trauma and social fear – not enough resources to give proper care.

CUE: BALLOONS OR FIREWORKS

(On AVERY's word 'care,' voices stop. Change of class bell - and then....a high school hallway – Monday afternoon. Snippets of sung conversation are heard)

VARIOUS STUDENTS/ENSEMBLE
(overlapping and repeating - solos at director's discretion)

DID YOU STUDY FOR THE QUIZ?
THE POINT IS TO SOLVE FOR "X"
MRS. FLETCHER JUST DOESN'T LIKE ME
WE BROKE UP LAST NIGHT SO PROM IS OFF
EL, ELLA, NOSOTROS, NOSOTRAS, VOSOTROS...
SORRY - I HAVE SOCCER AFTER SCHOOL
THIS PROBLEM IS IMPOSSIBLE
TWO PARTS HYDROGEN, ONE PART OXYGEN...
HOW DO I GET OUT OF GYM TODAY?
THOSE SHOES ARE SO CUTE
MY WEEKEND WAS A MESS – WAIT UNTIL YOU HEAR
(All together and overlapping)

VARIOUS STUDENTS/ENSEMBLE (CONT)
JUST GET TO 3:05
JUST GET TO 3:05
JUST SURVIVE TILL 3:0….

(BREAKING NEWS BULLETIN interrupts with music – on video or live)

NEWS ANCHOR (ON VIDEO OR REMOTE VOICE)

(During this announcement, the cast remains still and breathes audibly and in unison. Inhale then exhale…and with each sequence, the breathing increases in speed and intensity. Panic is setting in.)

This just coming in from our correspondents on the ground. We are receiving reports of an active shooter situation at Lincoln High School on the East Side of the city - it appears to be *(beat)* the, uh…*(to the correspondent)* what? Say it again - are you...*(back to broadcast)* yes...appears to be the Pine Street entrance… Reports are clearly varied and we do not wish to speculate but it appears that there may be multiple casualties among both students and faculty. The building is currently under lockdown. Parents are being urged to avoid the area surrounding the building while authorities work to stabilize the situation. Again - authorities are saying this situation is active and fluid. We are working to gather more details…and when we do…

(ANCHOR report fades as cast breathing becomes louder and overlapping and then…)

ENSEMBLE
ONE MISSISSIPPI
TWO MISSISSIPPI
THREE MISSISSIPPI
FOUR MISSISSIPPI
FIVE

(FACELESS THERAPIST interrupts)

THERAPIST
It's okay...take your time. Therapy is about healing and it
takes time....and reliving that day is hard - impossible, even
- so ... do only what you can.

ENSEMBLE (WITH SOLOS AT DIRECTOR'S DISCRETION)
IT SOUNDED LIKE SOMETHING DROPPED
LIKE IT POPPED - LIKE A BALLOON
OR LIKE FIREWORKS
LIKE THE FOURTH OF JULY
AND I WONDERED WHY
THERE WOULD BE FIREWORKS
SO SOON - BEFORE THE END OF JUNE
IT WAS ONLY MAY
MAYBE THAT WAS THE DELAY
AS IT ECHOED THROUGH THE STAIRWAY
ONE AFTER THE OTHER
AND ANOTHER
AND ANOTHER
I SHOULD'VE TEXTED MY MOTHER
OR CALLED 9-1-1
WHY DIDN'T I TEXT MY MOTHER?
WHY DIDN'T I CALL 9-1-1?
BUT LAST PERIOD WAS ALMOST DONE
BUT WHAT IF WHAT I HEARD WAS A ...

ENSEMBLE (ALL)
NO I COULDN'T IMAGINE
THERE'S A BADGE IN THE HALLWAY
AND A LAG IN MY MEMORY
AND I STILL CAN'T IMAGINE
NOT HERE
NOT AT LINCOLN
NOT TODAY
NOT TO US
NOT TO ME

SOLO ENSEMBLE MEMBER
Maybe I remember it wrong...or...I don't know...I'm sorry.

ENSEMBLE (ALL)
WILL I EVER SLEEP AGAIN
WILL I EVER FEEL AGAIN
WILL I EVER STOP WONDERING WHEN
MY LIFE RETURNS TO NORMAL
WILL ANYTHING BE NORMAL
WHAT IF THIS IS NORMAL?

(Chaos ensues and the day of the shooting is relived. NOTE: The song should focus on the aftermath and NEVER the shooter.)

ALL I KNOW IS IT WASN'T BALLOONS OR
FIREWORKS
IT WAS NEVER BALLOONS OR FIREWORKS
FIREWORKS
FIREWORKS
FIREWORKS

(Stop and...Beat....addressing faceless therapist)

WAS THERE ANYTHING ELSE YOU NEEDED?
I'VE SAID ALL I KNOW TO SAY

ENSEMBLE (ALL, CONT)
THE FLASHBACKS HAVE NOT RECEDED
AND I'D RATHER CALL IT A DAY

(Timer bell rings. Then faceless voice of therapist)

THERAPIST
Time's up. See you next week.

ENSEMBLE SOLOS
(Overlapping and fading)
THERE WAS A BADGE IN THE HALLWAY
THE POINT IS TO SOLVE FOR "X"
IT WASN'T A BALLOON
WE BROKE UP LAST NIGHT SO PROM IS OFF
WILL I EVER SLEEP AGAIN
I STILL CAN'T IMAGINE
WHY WOULD THERE BE FIREWORKS?

SOLO ENSEMBLE MEMBER
WHAT IF THIS IS...NORMAL?

ENSEMBLE (ALL)
NORMAL
NORMAL
NORMAL
NORMAL

AVERY
OK ENOUGH!

(Song ends. Long beat of AVERY calming herself after this overwhelming moment. She cannot process all of it scientifically...she becomes emotional. No underscore - just true raw

emotion from her. She eventually calms herself before she begins the next moment.)

SCENE 14 : A WAY OF LIFE

(ALICIA, ROSE, KRISTINA all split the stage in isolated light.
AVERY sits center in front of laptop.)

AVERY
(to Podcast Viewers - on screen)

Do you remember those memory matching games elementary school teachers would make you do? There would be something like – 20 cards on a table all facing down. The teacher you trusted so much would absolutely swear on their life that under those cards were images – an oak tree, a hummingbird, a fire truck – and the object of the game was to find the two cards with matching images – thus completing 10 pairs of matching cards. Easy, right? Except that if you flipped over a fire truck and a hummingbird, you had to turn them back over and start again – hoping your memory of that fire truck would come in handy when you found its match. I hated that game.

Case numbers 4811H, 4562H, and 4708H – all female – all seeing the same therapist - all showing near exact diagnoses, same therapy treatments and recovery patterns. But that, viewers, is where the comparison comes to an annoying, grinding halt. Case after case I keep reading – and every time I think I have found two fire trucks, here comes that damn hummingbird. I'm starting to worry that all 20 cards on the table have no match.

(NOTE: The following dialogue that leads to the song is a word-for-word account of real survivors. No word has been changed - just edited for time)

71

ROSE

I don't remember NOT having anxiety and depression.

ALICIA

I don't think I have a depression problem.

KRISTINA

Yeah - many would call me easily excitable and I have often been asked if I'm ever NOT smiling.

ROSE

My Dad suffered from depression before it was being diagnosed, so I know what it is like from both sides.

ALICIA

My mother is a strong woman, but to cope when my sister died, she just moved us around from school to school, apartment to apartment, even different states.

KRISTINA

Well that is the fake me. The 'me' I wished I was. It was like I was playing a role – 7 days a week – 2 matinees on the weekends for friends and family. But I think it was loneliness – the dark confining loneliness that led to me keeping the draft of the suicide note.

ROSE

I know a lot of people who've committed suicide. Well, anyway, I've only considered it.

ALICIA

Clinical depression, high anxiety, and a lot of self loathing... the pills make me sick and don't work at all. I generally hate myself and every day I wake up is another torture. But no – I would never kill myself. That's just stupid.

ROSE
Me? I don't know – I guess just to belong somewhere. That would make a difference for sure. But I don't know – I don't know what I want.

ALICIA
A friend. One fucking friend that sticks around through at least one birthday. Is that so much to ask?

CUE: HOME ENOUGH FOR ME

KRISTINA
I just wanna be better than before. Just someone – anyone to hear me. I don't need to be fixed – just heard.

IF I ASK YOU, WOULD YOU LISTEN?
IF I ASK YOU, WOULD YOU STAY
AND SHARE THIS BAG OF M&M'S WITH ME?
IF I WHISPER THAT THE DARKNESS WEIGHS ME DOWN TODAY
WOULD YOU TAKE ME TO A LIGHT THAT I CAN SEE?

ALICIA
IF I ASK YOU, WOULD YOU PLAY ME
THAT SONG THAT MAKES US DANCE
AND LAUGH UNTIL THE TEARS ROLL FROM OUR EYES

ROSE
IF I TELL YOU THAT I'M HURTING AND LOST AND COLD AND DONE
WILL YOU LIFT MY CHIN AND SHOW ME BRIGHTER SKIES

KRISTINA
I DON'T NEED A HOUSE – A ROOFTOP OR FOUR
WALLS
I DON'T NEED A FENCE, A LAWN OR SOME OLD
TREE
JUST A WALK, A TALK, A SONG, A CALL
A WORD OR TWO WHEN SPIRITS FALL
THAT WILL FEEL LIKE HOME ENOUGH TO ME

ALICIA
IF I ASK YOU, WOULD YOU LOVE ME
WHEN I'M FEELING LESS THAN LOVED
WOULD YOU SPLIT AN EXTRA LARGE CHEESE-
LOVER'S PIE

ROSE
WOULD YOU BINGE-WATCH SEASON 2 OF
"STRANGER THINGS"* JUST ONE MORE TIME
AND UNDERSTAND WHEN RANDOMLY I'LL CRY

***NOTE - This can change to reflect current viewing
popularity as long as the scan falls correctly - Change
must be approved by Uproar**

KRISTINA
IF I ASK YOU, WOULD YOU HEAR ME
IF I ASK YOU, WILL YOU HOLD

ALL
A PLACE FOR ME FOR WHEN I DON'T BELONG

ROSE
IF I TELL YOU I CAN'T DO THIS AND I START TO
BACK AWAY
WILL YOU TELL ME YOU'VE BEEN WITH ME ALL
ALONG

I DON'T NEED A HOUSE – A ROOFTOP OR FOUR
WALLS
I DON'T NEED A FENCE, A LAWN OR SOME OLD
TREE

ALICIA
JUST A WALK, A TALK, A SONG, A CALL
A WORD OR TWO WHEN SPIRITS FALL

KRISTINA
THAT WILL FEEL LIKE HOME ENOUGH TO ME

ALL
WHEN DARKNESS SETTLES IN LIKE A HAMMER
ON MY CHEST
YOU NEED SOMEONE WHO'S SEEN YOU AT
YOUR BEST
AND KNOWS THAT DARK IS JUST THE OTHER
SIDE OF LIGHT
AND WON'T LET YOU SLIP AWAY WITHOUT A
FIGHT

KRISTINA
I DON'T NEED A HOUSE – A ROOFTOP OR FOUR
WALLS

ALICIA
I DON'T NEED A FENCE

ROSE
A LAWN OR SOME OLD TREE

ALL
JUST A WALK, A TALK, A SONG, A CALL
A WORD OR TWO WHEN SPIRITS FALL
THAT WILL FEEL LIKE HOME ENOUGH TO ME
YOU WILL FEEL LIKE HOME ENOUGH TO ME

(blackout)

SCENE 15 – A PERSON COULD DEVELOP A COLD

> *(MAN 1 (AARON) and MAN 2 (MAX) are*
> *watching television – the CNN coverage of the*
> *supreme court decision on same-sex marriage.*
> *As the scene begins – MAX enters – getting*
> *ready to leave for work, breakfast, etc. – usual*
> *morning business. AVERY addresses audience.)*

AVERY
Case # 4591R. Archival. 2015.

AARON
Aaron.

AVERY
Extreme anxiety. Medication has controlled most of the
symptoms. Hypochondria manifests into paranoia at any
mention of going off the medication. Patient has responded
well to therapy.

MAX
You're going to be late for work. How many times are you
going to watch that?

AARON
I can't help it. I keep thinking it can't be true – like this
really didn't happen.

MAX
Well it did. And it happened yesterday. And I'm very excited.
But your need to DVR the news is beginning to worry to me.

AARON

Shut up. This is historic.

MAX

I know. I really do. I think it's cute. *(beat)* You know what this means?

AARON

I do...

MAX

And I do..

AARON

So are we…

MAX

Engaged?

AARON

I think we have been for a few years…We are like Adelaide and that dude from *Guys and Dolls*.

MAX

That DUDE from *Guys and Dolls*? I'm not sure which upsets me more – that you don't know his name or that you un-ironically used the phrase "that dude."

AARON

Unlike you, I didn't come out of the closet with an armful of cast recordings.

MAX

(faux shock) Then why come out at all! *(beat)* - So shall we set a date?

AARON

Now? I mean – I don't know. We don't need to rush into this
or...

MAX

Rush? Seriously...rush?

AARON

I just meant – we should think this through and weigh
options – Ya know what!? We should make a pros and cons
list. Yeah. *(Grabs paper and pencil)* One column for why we
SHOULD and one for...

> *(MAX sits next to AARON – takes the pencil and
> paper and takes his hands in his.)*

MAX

What is this about?

AARON

What do you mean? I just...

MAX

No really – what is going on with you?

AARON

What about my family? My job – I make shit salary – And
oh my God – what about YOUR Mom?

MAX

What is this *really* about?

AARON

Plus – everyone is going to do it right away now. Ours won't
be special. We should let the mass wedding exodus get out
of the way first, and then we can consider...

MAX

Is it this?

(he holds up a prescription bottle. beat…
AARON tries to say no –but he eventually –
slowly – nods yes)

CUE: WEATHERPROOF

AARON

I don't wanna marry you until I'm better….until I'm perfect.

MAX
(referencing the bottle)

THIS doesn't matter to me. THESE are not you. *(places his hand on AARON's heart).* THIS is you.

MAX

I NEVER WANTED PERFECT
JUST TO BE PERFECT FOR YOU
I NEVER ASKED FOR FOREVER
JUST FOR SOMETHING TO LOOK FORWARD TO
I NEVER NEEDED THIS
TO BE ENDLESS WEDDED BLISS
JUST YOU
JUST ME
AND AN HOUR OR TWO TOGETHER

BUT IN CASE I DON'T SAY ENOUGH
THAT YOU SEND ME TO THE MOON
IN CASE MY TEXTS AREN'T PROOF ENOUGH
THAT I SEND ALL AFTERNOON
AND JUST IN CASE YOU WONDER
ABOUT THE SPELL YOU'VE GOT ME UNDER
NO AMOUNT OF RAIN COULD BRING ME ANY
PAIN
YOU'VE MADE MY LIFE WEATHERPROOF

AARON

But I need these – without them I am not …me.

MAX

That's bullshit – and you know it. Maybe you DO need them
– and maybe you don't. Either way – it's never going to
change what I feel – what YOU feel…Do you love me?

AARON

Of course I love you..

MAX

I don't need anything else….what about you?

AARON

No…No, I don't.

BOTH

LIGHTNING MAY STRIKE AND HAIL WILL FALL
NOTHING FOR ME WOULD CHANGE AT ALL
WIND AND RAIN AND ICE AND SNOW
AND STILL I ALWAYS KNOW…THE THINGS I
KNOW

AARON

FLOOD AND MUDSLIDE – I COULD TAKE

MAX

THERE'S SO MUCH MORE FOR US AT STAKE

BOTH

BRING THE TWISTER AND TYPHOON
THAT DAY WITH YOU CAN'T COME TOO SOON
I WILL NOT MOVE WITH TREPIDATION
JUST TO AVOID A LITTLE PRECIPITATION

AARON
SO IN CASE I DON'T SAY ENOUGH
THAT YOU SEND ME TO THE MOON

MAX
IN CASE MY TEXTS AREN'T PROOF ENOUGH
THAT I SEND ALL AFTERNOON

BOTH
AND JUST IN CASE YOU WONDER
ABOUT THE SPELL YOU'VE GOT ME UNDER
NO AMOUNT OF RAIN COULD BRING ME ANY
PAIN
NO NO – NO AMOUNT OF RAIN COULD BRING
US ANY PAIN
YOU'VE MADE MY LIFE WEATHERPROOF

MAX
And by the way – Adelaide and 'that dude' get married at the
end of *Guys and Dolls.*

AARON
Well it's about damn time.

(Final chord rings. Blackout.)

SCENE 16: ANOTHER EPISODE

AVERY

*(AVERY is recording another podcast episode.
She is exhausted.)*

…and once the files start aligning a bit more, I think I'll be
ready to make some assertions about next steps and where

the research is leading in terms of …well finding an end
game, as it were. There seems to be no real correlation…

(AVERY's phone rings.)

Um....between the…

> *(AVERY hits pause on recording. Takes the call.*
> *MACY appears)*

AVERY

Hey! What's up?

MACY

Hey..

AVERY

Are you OK or…*(beat)*….

MACY

Can you come home today?

AVERY

Well no…I mean – maybe Saturday but I can't leave right…
(beat)…

MACY

'Cause it's happening again –

AVERY

What's happening?

MACY

…and I'm freaking out – and no one…

AVERY

Mace - WHAT is happening?

MACY

One of those...episodes...I told you!

AVERY

Ok, listen…*(AVERY grabs a file folder, flips through to a specific page)* So do you feel that any of these symptoms are accurate: racing heart, dizziness, tingling in the extremities, chest pains,...

MACY

Are you reading that right now??

AVERY

Macy, listen - on a scale from 1-10…

MACY

Are you actually pulling your doctor bullshit on me?

AVERY

(drops the folder..a little panicked..changes course)
Maybe...just breathe...you should breathe.

MACY

That's your big solution? Breathe?? I am breathing, Ave…

AVERY

No – I know you're breathing…I'm just saying...

MACY

(frustrated) Just...um...know what? You're right. I'll be fine. Saturday, then. *(beat)*...

AVERY

Where's Mom?...

MACY

Abandoned house, sis. Abandoned house. I gotta go.

AVERY

Ok so is there anyone you can call? A friend or...?

MACY

I did, Ave. I just fucking did.

> *(and immediately she's off the phone. AVERY tries her back. No answer. Blackout.)*

SCENE 17: THE FIRST CUT IS THE DEEPEST

> *(AVERY is in the middle of recording a particularly lengthy podcast episode. She has come to a conclusion.)*

AVERY

Linking these cases has become a priority at this point. This essentially means I need to start doing some psych evaluations with real live patents. So I started by attending a recovery meeting for one of the cases. Case number 3288L...very, very ongoing.

> *(WOMAN 2 (AMY) steps to a podium and microphone.She is nervous. What she is about to do is very difficult for her)*

AMY

Hi. Um...I'm Amy.

AVERY

She reminded me of Macy – this one was unexpectedly harder for me.

AMY

> *(Clears her throat – addresses the meeting attendees – nervous and unaccustomed to speaking in front of anyone – let alone about herself. Tests the mic and then…)*

It's been about 3 months since God began to free me from self-harm for good but I still think about it….a lot actually.

CUE: RELYING ON THE KNIFE

Cutting is...was... a way for me to find release for the anger and stress that I worked so hard to keep bottled up. Other times – it was to just feel SOMETHING – anything at all. Pain was at least a feeling. Numbness is like a death – that you keep re-living. And my cutting? Well – I re-live those nights every day in vivid fucking detail.

> *(We are back with AMY on one of those dark nights of self-harm)*

ONE STEP AT A TIME
BREATHING LIKE THE PAMPHLET TELLS YOU TO
ONE MISSISSIPPI
TWO MISSISSIPPI
THREE MISSISSIPPI
FOUR MISSISSIPPI
FIVE

> *(beat)*

AMY (CONT)

(Spoken) Nothing changed…try again

ONE MISSISSIPPI
TWO MISSISSIPPI
THREE MISSISSIPPI
FOUR MISSISSIPPI
BREATHING REMINDS ME THAT I'M NOT YET
DEAD
BUT I'M SEARCHING FOR PROOF - PROOF I'M
ALIVE

SEE – CUTS JUST NEED BAND-AIDS
AND BLOOD JUST DRAINS AWAY
AND THEN IT'S GONE
AND THEN IT'S GONE
I CAN DO BAND-AIDS
AND WATER TO WASH AWAY
THAT MAKES SENSE TO ME
THIS MAKES SENSE TO ME
AND SO I WASH AWAY THE PAIN OF LIFE
RELYING ON THE KNIFE
HURT IS ALL I FEEL NOW
THE ONLY WAY TO TELL
IF I'M STILL BREATHING
AM I STILL BREATHING?
THIS MAY BE THE ONLY WAY
TO CHECK IF I'M OKAY:
MY PULSE IS BEATING
MY HEART IS BLEEDING

I DON'T KNOW WHO THIS GIRL IS – THIS FACE
IN THE MIRROR
TOO FAR GONE FOR LESSONS TO TEACH
CAUSE THE BLEEDING SHE'S FEELING IS NOT
FROM HER SKIN

BUT FROM SOMEWHERE INSIDE SHE CAN'T
REACH
THE BLEEDING INSIDE CAN'T BE REACHED

ONE MISSISSIPPI
TWO MISSISSIPPI
THREE MISSISSIPPI
FOUR MISSISSIPPI
FIVE
THAT MAKES SENSE TO ME
THIS MAKES SENSE TO ME
BUT HOW LONG CAN THIS BE MY LIFE
RELYING ON THE KNIFE

> *(AMY gathers herself – realizes where she is
> again.)*

So yeah….um. That's my story.

> *(Segue. Final chord. Immediate segue to song.)*

SCENE 18: DAYS LIKE THIS

CUE: GOOD.FINE.OK.

> *(AVERY – frantic – feeling lost – sits amid stacks
> of papers, typing away – writing notes,
> deciphering interviews. Her frustration is
> growing. She's hearing voices of her case files.
> They overlap to a cacophony.*
>
> *All actors have appeared and begin layered the
> repeating of case numbers over and over and
> over again until the vocal begins breaking the
> noise.)*

SOLO 1

SO IT'S DAYS LIKE THIS I'M NOT SURE WHAT
I'M THINKING
AND WHETHER I'LL SURVIVE ANOTHER ROUND
SO I WANDER IN A FOG – AND FEEL I'M SINKING
STRUGGLING TO KEEP MY FEET ON THE
GROUND
THIS MAY BE THE LAST DAY I CAN TAKE
BEFORE I HAVE MY MENTAL BREAK
WAIT - JUST TAKE A BREATH, THEY SAY
ALL IS GOOD. IT IS FINE. IT'LL BE OK.

SOLO 2

I SHOULD HAVE KNOWN TODAY IT WOULD BE
RAINING
JUST WHEN I SO BADLY NEEDED SUN
I KNOW I HAVE NO RIGHT TO BE COMPLAINING
JUST COUNT BACKWARDS – TEN BACK DOWN
TO ONE
I SHOULD HAVE SPENT THE DAY IN BED
ESCAPING FROM WHAT'S IN MY HEAD
BUT SOMEHOW I'LL SURVIVE THE GLOOM AND
GRAY
ALL IS GOOD.

SOLO 1

IT IS FINE

BOTH

IT'LL BE OK.

ALL

NO NEED FOR PANIC
FOR FRANTIC
OR MANIC THINKING
IT'S ALL IN YOUR HEAD
IT'S ALL IN YOUR HEAD

ALL (CONT)
IT'S ALL IN YOUR HEAD
IT'S ALL IN YOUR HEAD
IT'S ALL IN MY…

SOLO 3
SO HERE I AM – THE WORLD FEELS LIKE IT'S
SPINNING
I COULD VOMIT - GOD IT SUCKS TO BE THIS
SCARED

SOLO 4
JUST ANOTHER DAY I'M SURE I WON'T BE
WINNING I WOULD SETTLE JUST TO FEEL THAT
SOMEONE CARED

SOLO 3
IT'S TOO LATE TO GO HOME I GUESS

SOLO 4
CAUSE EVERYTHING I TOUCH IS A MESS

BOTH
ANOTHER CHANCE TO SCREW THINGS UP
AGAIN ALL IS GOOD. IT IS FINE. IT'LL BE …

ALL
OH NO – NOT TODAY
I CANNOT FEEL THIS WAY
CAN'T LET IT PASS – IGNORE IT, TOO
THE CRAZY HAS A WAY OF LEAKING THROUGH
THE CRAZY IS THE ONLY THING THAT'S
GETTING THROUGH

SOLO 5
IT'S ALL IN YOUR HEAD

SOLO 6
IT'S ALL IN YOUR HEAD

BOTH
IT'S ALL IN YOUR HEAD

ALL
THE PROBLEM HERE IS ALL JUST IN MY HEAD

SOLO 1
THIS MAY BE THE LAST DAY I CAN TAKE

SOLO 2
I SHOULD'VE SPENT THE DAY IN BED

SOLO 3
I COULD VOMIT – GOD IT SUCKS TO BE THIS
SCARED

SOLO 4
I'D SETTLE JUST TO FEEL THAT SOMEONE
CARED

ALL
ALL IS GOOD. ALL IS FINE
ALL IS GOOD. ALL IS FINE.
ALL IS GOOD. ALL IS FINE. IT'LL BE OK.
IT'LL BE OK.
ALL IS GOOD. ALL IS FINE. IT'LL BE OK.
IT'LL BE OK. IT'LL BE OK.

*(AVERY has had enough. Voices and actors
immediately go away.)*

CUE: CLARITY/CONFUSION

AVERY/MACY
OK
OK ENOUGH
OK ENOUGH ALREADY

AVERY
I GET IT – I HEAR YOU
BUT I STILL DON'T UNDERSTAND
NO I STILL DON'T UNDER…
WAIT…ALL IS GOOD. IT IS FINE. IT'LL BE OK.
THIS IS NOT OK

MACY
I AM NOT OK…

(Avery files through her paperwork – her research)

AVERY
SEE I DID ALL THE RESEARCH
I FOLLOWED THE RULES
I CHARTED THE PROGRESS WITH ALL OF THE
TOOLS
I'D BEEN GIVEN
SPREADSHEETS AND PIE CHARTS
NAME AFTER NAME
DECADES OF STUDIES FROM EXPERTS WHO
CLAIM
TO KNOW MORE – THAN EVER BEFORE

AND I THOUGHT FACTS WOULD PAINT THE
PICTURE
AND I THOUGHT NUMBERS DIDN'T LIE
I THOUGHT MEDICINE ALONE WOULD CURE
THE ACHE
AND HEAL WHAT BROKE INSIDE
BUT THE DIVISION MULTIPLIES THE FALL

AVERY (CONT)
AND THE NUMBERS DON'T ADD UP AT ALL
SO WE MEASURE OUR LIVES IN COMMENTS
AND POSTS
AND END UP LIVING WITH OUR GHOSTS

(Suddenly, AVERY grabs file folder after file folder with charts. She scours through her files frantically searching for things she missed or avoided.)

MACY
OUR WORLD WAS A GIANT FORT OF BLANKETS
PLAYING TRUTH OR DARE
I'D GIVE ANYTHING FOR ANOTHER DAY
LIKE THE ONES WE HAD BACK THEN…
ONE MISSISSIPPI
TWO MISSISSIPPI
THREE MISSISSIPPI
FOUR MISSISSIPPI
FIVE

AVERY

(For each of the following lines, AVERY opens a new one before discarding it. This line should overlap MACY's counting)

Look! Does my professor want numbers? Here are some numbers!

EIGHT IS THE AGE THAT EMMA STARTED
CUTTING
ZERO IS THE NUMBER OF TIMES SHE ASKED
FOR HELP
SEVEN IS THE NUMBER OF DAYS A WEEK PAUL
DRINKS

AVERY (CONT)
AND PRAYS HE WON'T SURVIVE THE DRIVE
BACK HOME
I DON'T HOW TO MEASURE HER PAIN
I DON'T HOW TO CALCULATE HIS SHAME

(More files, more frantic than ever, AVERY looks for answers. MACY on a stretcher being taken away by EMT's)

MACY
IT'S LIKE YEARS OF WORDS READY TO…
READY TO…
BOTH ME AND VODKA ON THE ROCKS
THE TIME IN ENDLESS TICKS AND TOCKS
TICK TOCK, TICK TOCK, TICK TOCK
HITTING THE WALL
FEELING THE FALL
IT'S THE LAST…
THE LAST CALL

(AVERY's phone rings. She answers.)

AVERY
Yes – of course. This is Avery. What? I mean, yes...yes. Wait I don't understand what you're *(enters panic mode - her sister is in crisis)* … well yes, she's my sister – I'm on my way.

(She grabs her keys and is off.)

SCENE 19 – GETTING HELP

(AVERY enters a hospital hallway barely looking up – frantically moving from room to room. She

sees MACY - and sees evidence of Macy's attempt, whether bandaged wrists or neck, etc.)

AVERY
Oh, Macy. What - I mean…

MACY
Avery? What are you…I mean how did you know I was here…or that... Did they tell you? Oh God – tell me they didn't tell you.

AVERY
Why am I here, Macy? Why are YOU here?

(beat. They are both silent. MACY turns away eventually – embarrassed.)

MACY
We don't all have our shit together, sis.

AVERY
That's not what I meant.

MACY
Who called you? How did you know…?

AVERY
The hospital, Macy. The hospital called me.

(Beat. It all starts to sink in.)

AVERY
I must be your emergency contact -

MACY

Fucking perfect. Well, Ave - dream come true for you, isn't it? You get to psychoanalyze me and figure me out, right? A real live patient! And I'm super broken - so this should get you an A on the final, I would think.

AVERY

I'm not doing this…I'm here as your sister, not ...

MACY

No no – let's do this. Let the healing begin! Here I'll get us started. Page one – acute personality disorder, mood swings indicative of trauma-triggered anxiety – How am I doing, Doc?

AVERY

Macy stop - this is not….

(AVERY just wants out of there)

MACY

Potential mild schizophrenia with tendencies toward paranoia and manic behavior. And here's my favorite part, Doc – multiple life attempts. Haha. What does that even mean? Cause what it should say is "patient failed at ending her fucking existence on three different occasions." That's more accurate, don't you think?

(AVERY runs to her and interrupts her long enough to take her in his arms)

MACY

I'm sorry I didn't tell you. I'm sorry...

AVERY

Shut up. Just shut up.

(Take the beat here. Make sure this moment gets some love)

MACY
I'm scared. I don't wanna do this alone.

AVERY
And you don't *have* to now, do you...

MACY
What happens next?

CUE: BACK THEN (REPRISE)

AVERY
(slowly...to be sure MACY understands)
Listen – you aren't gonna be able to leave right now…

(MACY starts to panic)

MACY
ONE MISSISSIPPI
TWO MISSISSIPPI
THREE MISSISSIPPI
FOUR MISSISSIPPI
FIVE...

AVERY
I know it's…

MACY
(spiraling)
No, no, no… They're gonna take me away, Ave. Listen - we can go home and see Mom - and we'll all talk and ...we got this, right? I mean - this is just a bump...we can handle a bump...

AVERY

No. This is it. I know this is huge – but you have to do this.
I'll stay with you.

MACY

I can't stay here...I am not going to make it if I have to...

AVERY

*(Getting into the hospital bed with her. Holds
her. Their physical interaction is intense and
somewhat violent even.)*
Don't think about-- just...

MACY

I will murder you if you tell me to breathe...

AVERY

YOU AND I IN PJ'S

Remember?

WHISPERING ALL NIGHT

Think about you and me, Mace.

PLANNING FUTURES TOGETHER
BY THE LIGHT OF THE FLASHLIGHT
HOW WE'D GIVE ANYTHING FOR ANOTHER DAY
LIKE THE ONES WE HAD BACK THEN

MACY

Those days are long gone...

AVERY

But WE'RE still here.

AVERY
OUR WORLD WAS A GIANT FORT OF BLANKETS
PLAYING TRUTH OR DARE
NO TOPIC WAS OFF-LIMITS
NO WORDS WE COULDN'T SHARE

AVERY/MACY
I LOVED US AS A PAIR

MACY
I DON'T KNOW HOW TO GET BACK THERE

AVERY
We'll find it together.

CAUSE I LOVE WHO YOU WERE AND WHO YOU
STILL ARE

MACY
I NEVER MEANT TO DRIFT SO FAR

AVERY
I know.

MACY
I can't promise I won't try again. I can't. What if this never
gets better? What if I'm not cured?

AVERY
You might *not* be cured, Macy – but you *will* be better.
That's all I know for sure.

AVERY
YOU AND I TOGETHER

MACY
YOU AND I TOGETHER

BOTH
DOING WHAT WE DO
FINDING WHAT IS TRUE
WE'LL SURVIVE THIS TOO

MACY
We?

AVERY
Yes…we.

AVERY/MACY
THE WAY WE WERE BACK THEN
THE WAY WE WERE BACK THEN
YOU AND I CAN BE THAT WAY AGAIN

MACY
But what if…

(AVERY grabs her hands tightly)

AVERY
You can't live in "what if." Trust me…I've tried. For once –
let's try "what is" and go from there.

MACY
Peasy?

AVERY
Peasy.

(Button. Blackout)

SCENE 20: FIGHTING THE FIGHT

(All ensemble actors appear as they did in the opening scene – in isolated moments. One by one – as the vocal begins - they hand their file back to AVERY – all except MACY – almost ceremoniously.)

CUE: PORCH LIGHT

AVERY
I KNOW ONE DAY YOU'LL FIND YOUR WAY
BACK TO ME
NO MATTER HOW LONG

AVERY AND ONE ENSEMBLE MEMBER
I KNOW YOU THINK THAT I WENT AWAY WHEN
LIFE FELL APART

AVERY AND TWO ENSEMBLE MEMBERS
YOU COULDN'T BE MORE WRONG

ALL
(without Macy)
I ONLY EVER WANTED TO BE THERE FOR YOU –
CARE FOR YOU
LIKE I SAID I WOULD DO – LIKE I SAID I WOULD
DO
LIKE I AM SUPPOSED TO DO
BUT I NEED TO SEE THIS THROUGH – AND HELP
YOU SEE
AND LEAVE THE PORCH LIGHT ON FOR WHEN
YOU'RE NEEDING ME
FIND YOUR WAY – FIGHT THIS FIGHT
AND WHEN YOU FEEL IT'S TOO DARK TO SEE
LET THE PORCH LIGHT LEAD YOU BACK TO ME
HMMMM….

(during humming verse, we see MACY sitting across from AVERY)

AVERY

How about I walk you through what they will ask you.

MACY

How about we leave.

(AVERY looks at her as if to imply "wrong answer...try again")

MACY

Ok...yes. I know. You're right. Geez...I feel sorry for your future patients, you hardass!

AVERY
(laughing)

Yeah...sometimes so do I.

MACY

So lay it on me, Doctor.

AVERY

On a scale from 1-5. One being "never" and 5 being "always," answer the following questions. How often do you feel anxious, worried or scared?

MACY
(thinks)

3.

AVERY

How often do you have trouble sleeping?

MACY

2 or...maybe 3.

AVERY

How often do you despair – to the point of wishing harm upon yourself?

MACY

2.

AVERY

And lastly - at present, how often in the last 3 months, have you made plans for or attempts at self harm?

MACY
(breathes)

One… just one.

(AVERY smiles. MACY smiles. The evaluation continues but silently as the music swells.)

ENSEMBLE
I COULD BE YOUR 'HERE NOW'
I COULD BE YOUR 'LONG GONE'
I COULD BE YOUR GLASS OF LEMONADE
I COULD BE YOUR STREET SIGN
I COULD BE YOUR DETOUR
I COULD BE THE ONE WHO ALWAYS STAYED –
STAYED - STAYED

(AVERY hands MACY back her file. They join the ENSEMBLE.)

BUT I NEED TO SEE THIS THROUGH – AND HELP YOU SEE
AND LEAVE THE PORCH LIGHT ON FOR WHEN YOU'RE NEEDING ME FIND YOUR WAY – FIGHT THIS FIGHT
AND WHEN YOU FEEL IT'S TOO DARK TO SEE
LET THE PORCH LIGHT LEAD YOU BACK TO ME

ENSEMBLE (CONT)
WHEN YOU FEEL IT'S TOO DARK
LET THE PORCH LIGHT LEAD YOU BACK TO ME

MACY
This almost had a different ending.

AVERY
I know.

MACY
...but because of you...

AVERY
Because of *you,* Macy…and this step is...brave...it's huge.

CUE: RISE

MACY
So...what now?

AVERY
There's a blanket in the bathtub, I mean if you…

MACY
I'll take it.

I'VE GROWN ACCUSTOMED TO THE RAIN
HOW HARD IT FALLS AND HOW IT CALLS OUT
MY PAIN I'VE KNOWN HOW SHAME CAN
DARKEN SKIES
WHEN TRUTH SETS IN IT'S HARD TO SEE
BEYOND THE LIES BUT I WON'T LET CLOUDS
DISTRACT MY VIEW
LONG AS I'VE GOT YOU
WE CAN STAND UP AND BE SEEN. WE'LL…

MACY (CONT)

RISE
FROM THE DEPTHS THE STRUGGLE TAKES US
TO
WE RISE
WITH THE STRENGTH WE HAVE IN ME AND YOU
LIKE A PHOENIX FROM THE ASHES
ROARING STRONG LIKE THUNDER CRASHES
WE RISE
RISE
WE WILL RISE

ENSEMBLE (with solos at director discretion)

I'VE GROWN USED TO WORDS OF HATE
A GATHERED CROWD ALL SHOUTING LOUD
AND THROWING WEIGHT BUT I KNOW THE
SOUND REBELLION MAKES
LIFTED HIGH – ACROSS THE SKY – IT RIPPLES
AND QUAKES AND THE TIME HAS COME TO
MAKE IT HEARD
BIT BY BIT, WORD BY WORD

ENSEMBLE (ALL)

WE WILL STAND UP AND BE SEEN. WE'LL…
RISE
FROM THE DEPTHS THE STRUGGLE TAKES US
TO
WE RISE
WITH THE STRENGTH WE HAVE IN ME AND YOU
LIKE A PHOENIX FROM THE ASHES
ROARING STRONG LIKE THUNDER CRASHES
WE RISE
RISE

SOLOS BUILDING TO FULL ENSEMBLE

I AM WORTHY
I AM WORTHY

SOLOS BUILDING TO FULL ENSEMBLE (CONT)
I DON'T HAVE TO FEEL THE SHAME OR TAKE
THE BLAME
YES I AM WORTHY
I AM WORTHY
I DON'T HAVE TO FEEL THE SHAME OR TAKE
THE BLAME OR TAKE THE BLAME…

ENSEMBLE (ALL)
WE RISE
FROM THE DEPTHS THE STRUGGLE TAKES US
TO
WE RISE
WITH THE STRENGTH WE HAVE IN ME AND YOU
LIKE A PHOENIX FROM THE ASHES
ROARING STRONG LIKE THUNDER CRASHES
WE RISE
RISE
WE WILL RISE, RISE
WITH ASSURANCE IN OUR EYES
RISE, RISE
AMID THE SOUND OF DEAFENING CRIES
NOT ONE LIFE IS LEFT FORSAKEN
NOT ONE ROAD IS LEFT UNTAKEN
TOGETHER WE RISE (LIKE A PHOENIX FROM
THE ASHES) TOGETHER WE RISE (ROARING
STRONG LIKE THUNDER CRASHES) WE RISE
WE RISE
WE WILL RISE

(Blackout. End of play.)